W9-AJM-285

True Stories of WORLD WAR I

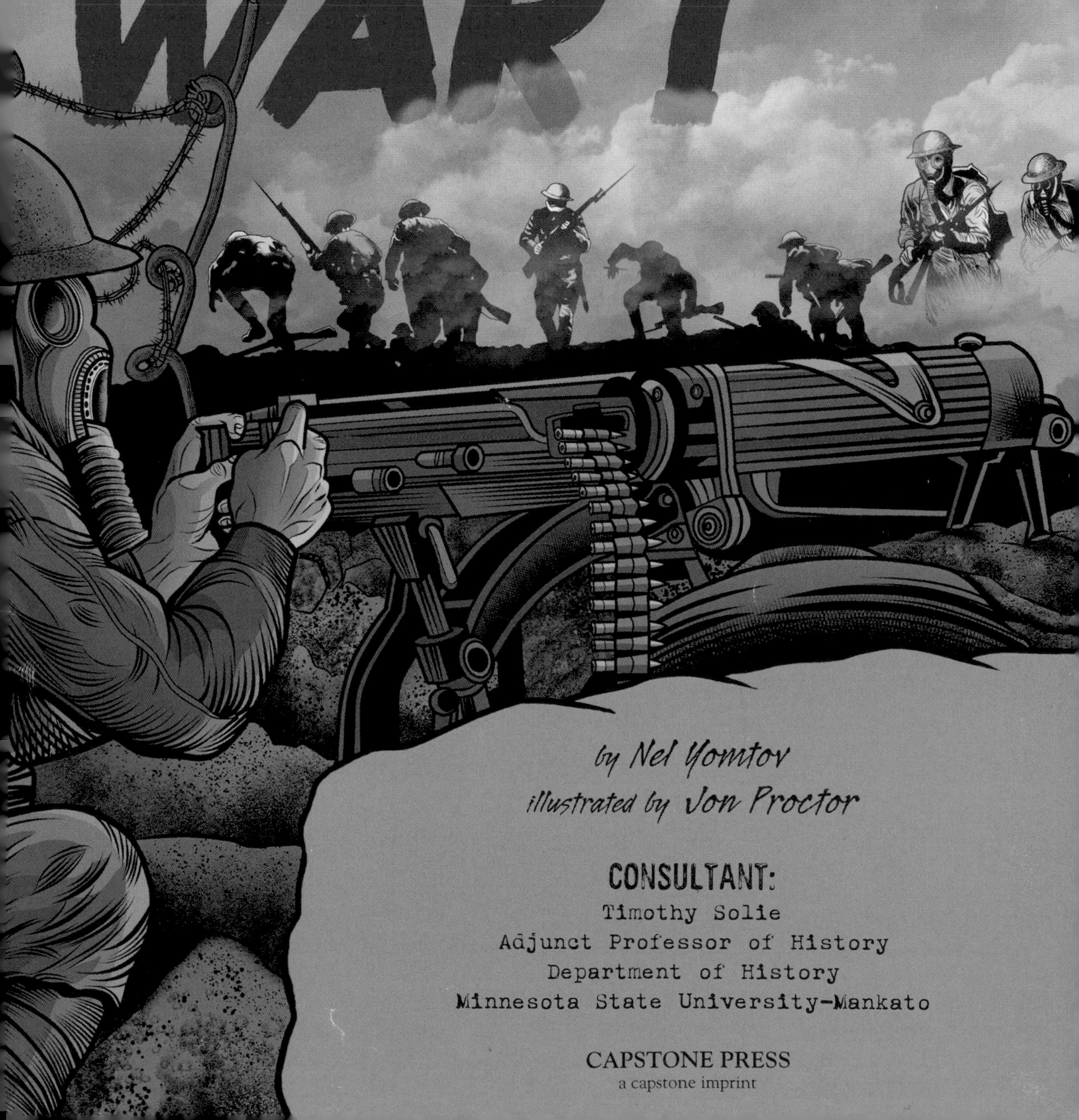

by Nel Yomtov

illustrated by Jon Proctor

CONSULTANT:

Timothy Solie
Adjunct Professor of History
Department of History
Minnesota State University-Mankato

CAPSTONE PRESS
a capstone imprint

Graphic Library is published by Capstone Press,
1710 Roe Crest Drive
North Mankato, Minnesota 56003
www.capstonepub.com

Library of Congress Cataloging-in-Publication Data
Yomtov, Nelson.
True stories of World War I / by Nel Yomtov ; illustrated by Jon Proctor.
p. cm.—(Graphic library. Stories of war)
Includes bibliographical references and index.
Summary: "In graphic novel format, tells the stories of six men who fought for their countries during World War I"—Provided by publisher.
ISBN 978-1-4296-8625-9 (library binding)
ISBN 978-1-4296-9344-8 (paperback)
ISBN 978-1-62065-270-1 (ebook PDF)
1. World War, 1914-1918—Biography—Juvenile literature.
2. Soldiers—Biography—Juvenile literature. I. Proctor, Jon, 1974- ill. II. Title.
D507.Y66 2013
940.40092'2-dc23 2011051832

EDITOR: Christopher L. Harbo

DESIGNER: Ashlee Suker

ART DIRECTOR: Nathan Gassman

PRODUCTION SPECIALIST: Laura Manthe

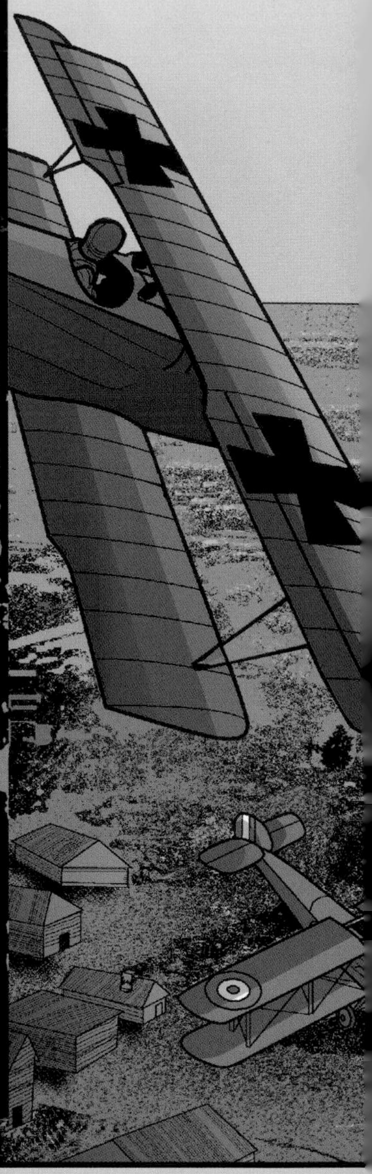

Editor's note: Direct quotations from primary sources are indicated by green text.

Direct quotations appear on the following pages:
Pages 7, 8, 9 from *A Student in Arms* by Donald Hankey (New York: E.P. Dutton & Co., 1917).
Page 14 from *Letters and Diary of Alan Seeger* by Alan Seeger (New York: C. Scribner's Sons, 1917).
Page 17 from *Poems* by Alan Seeger (New York: C. Scribner's Sons, 1916).
Pages 20-21 from "The Diary of Alvin York" by Alvin York, http://acacia.pair.com/Acacia.Vignettes/The.Diary.of.Alvin.York.html
Page 28 from *Over the Top* by Arthur Guy Empey (New York: G.P. Putnam's Sons, 1917).

Printed in the United States of America in Stevens Point, Wisconsin.
122012 007083R

TABLE OF CONTENTS

WORLD WAR I: THE GREAT WAR

Even for people who didn't live through it, World War I (1914–1918) is known as the Great War. Never before had two alliances of the world's most powerful nations clashed in mortal combat. The Allied powers included Great Britain, France, Russia, Belgium, and later the United States. The Central powers mainly included Germany, Austria-Hungary, and the Ottoman Empire.

The assassination of Archduke Franz Ferdinand by a Bosnian-Serb in June 1914 sparked the conflict. Ferdinand was in line for the Austria-Hungary throne. The shooter was a member of a revolutionary movement. He wanted the Serbian people to form a nation independent from Austria-Hungary.

One month later, the flames of war erupted in full. Austria-Hungary invaded Serbia. Germany then invaded Belgium, Luxembourg, and France. Russia attacked Germany. Fighting then broke out in Italy, Bulgaria, Romania, and in Pacific Ocean territories. For years the United States tried to stay out of the war. But in 1917 Germany's attacks on American commercial ships bound for Britain could not be ignored. The United States joined the war.

In November 1918 Germany, the only remaining Central power left fighting, agreed to a cease-fire. After four years of bloody combat, more than 35 million soldiers and civilians were dead, wounded, or missing.

Many soldiers kept diaries and journals about their experiences during the war. Get ready to explore six personal accounts of brave soldiers from both sides of the conflict.

Key Dates of World War I

JUNE 1914: Archduke Franz Ferdinand is assassinated.

AUGUST 1914: Germany declares war on France and Belgium. Britain declares war on Germany. Austria-Hungary declares war on Russia.

SEPTEMBER 1914: Allied forces win the First Battle of the Marne near Paris, France.

OCTOBER-NOVEMBER 1914: Allied forces win the First Battle of Ypres in Belgium.

MAY 1915: A German U-boat sinks the British passenger liner *Lusitania*, killing 1,198 civilians.

APRIL 1915-MAY 1916: The Central powers win the Gallipoli Campaign in Turkey.

FEBRUARY-DECEMBER 1916: Allied forces win the Battle of Verdun in France.

JULY-NOVEMBER 1916: The Battle of the Somme is fought to a draw in France.

APRIL 1917: The United States declares war on Germany.

JULY-AUGUST 1918: Allied forces win the Second Battle of the Marne in France.

NOVEMBER 1918: Germany agrees to a cease-fire, ending the war.

MAJOR ALLIED AND CENTRAL POWERS

USA
NORWAY
SWEDEN
Moscow
North Sea
DENMARK
GREAT BRITAIN
Baltic Sea
RUSSIA
London
NETH.
Berlin
BELG.
GERMAN EMPIRE
Paris
Vienna
ATLANTIC OCEAN
FRANCE
AUSTRIA-HUNGARY
ROMANIA
Black Sea
PORT.
ITALY
SERBIA
SPAIN
Corsica (Fr.)
Rome
BULGARIA
Mallorca (Sp.)
MONTENEGRO
OTTOMAN EMPIRE
Sardinia (It.)
ALB.
Mediterranean Sea
GREECE
SP. MOROCCO
Sicily
ALGERIA (Fr.)
TUNISIA (Fr.)
Crete
Cyprus (Br.)

Allied Powers
Central Powers
Neutral nations

CH. 2

Donald Hankey: Baptism by Fire

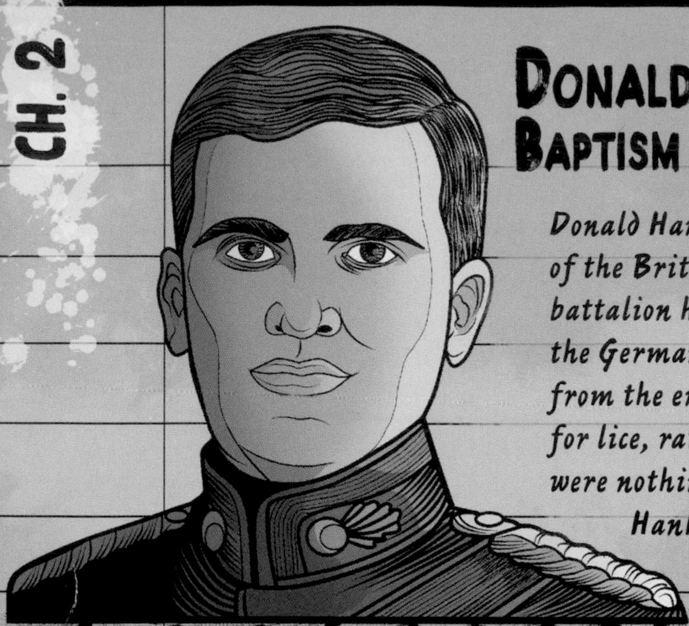

Donald Hankey was a sergeant in the 7th Battalion of the British Rifle Brigade. In 1915 Hankey's battalion held trenches that had been captured from the Germans. These trenches offered protection from the enemy, but they were also breeding grounds for lice, rats, and disease. But the awful conditions were nothing compared to the battle that awaited Hankey and his fellow soldiers.

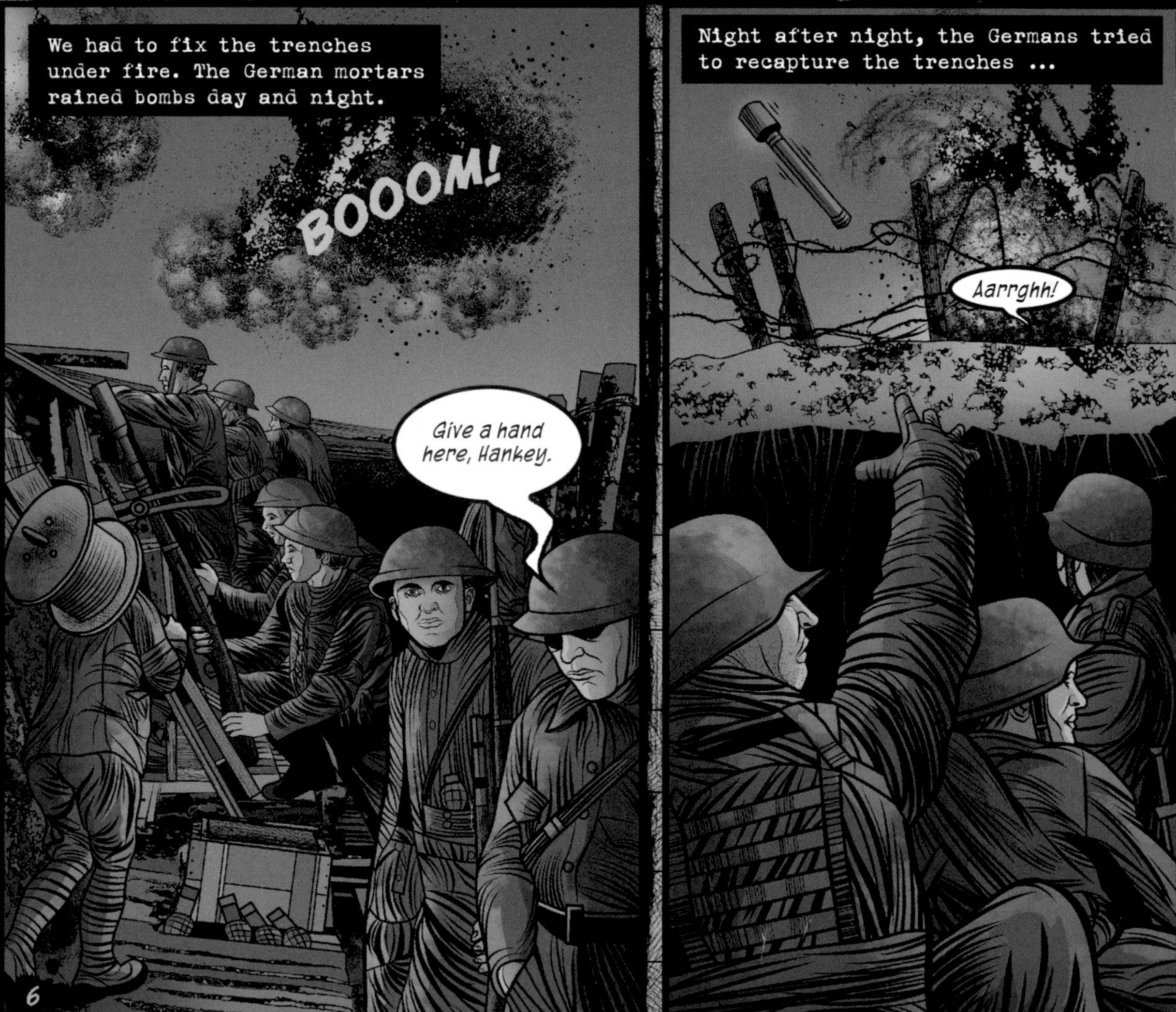

We had to fix the trenches under fire. The German mortars rained bombs day and night.
BOOOM!
Give a hand here, Hankey.
Night after night, the Germans tried to recapture the trenches ...
Aarrghh!

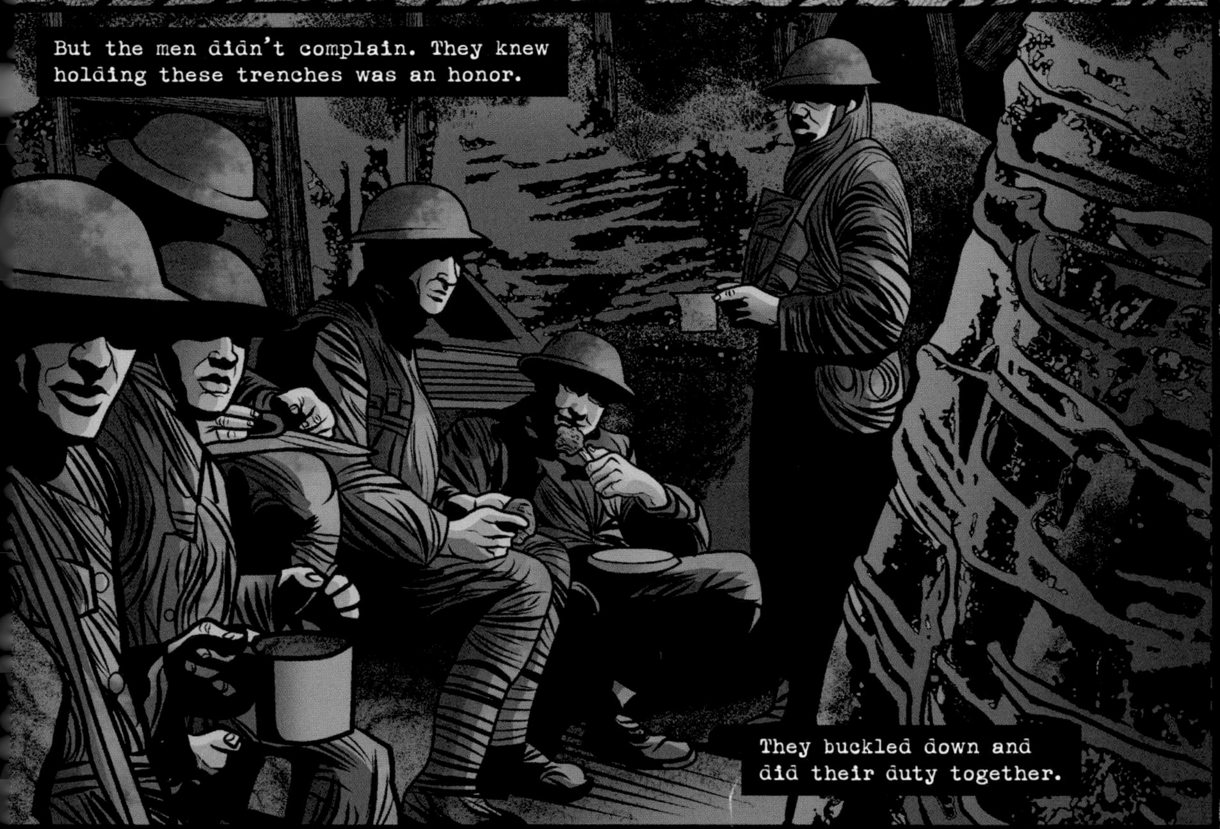
But the men didn't complain. They knew holding these trenches was an honor.
They buckled down and did their duty together.

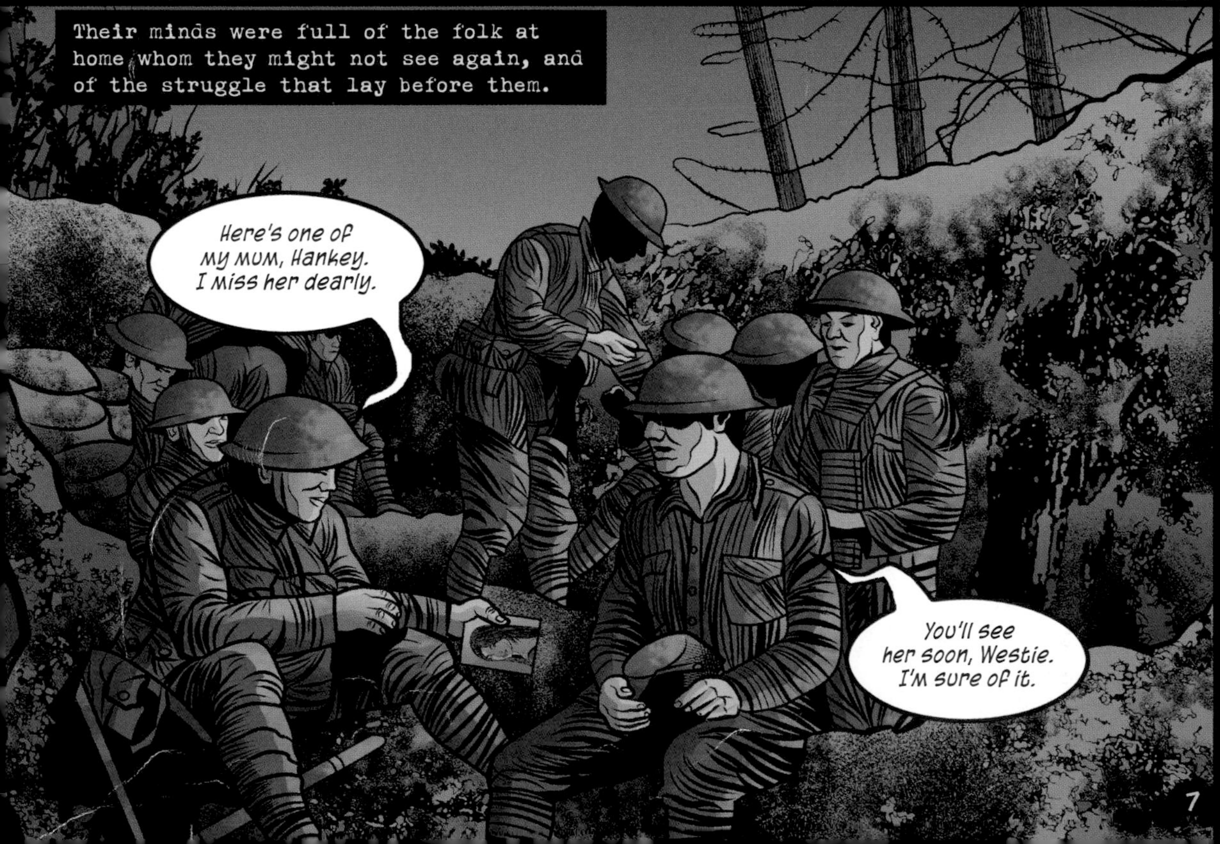
Their minds were full of the folk at home whom they might not see again, and of the struggle that lay before them.
Here's one of my mum, Hankey. I miss her dearly.
You'll see her soon, Westie. I'm sure of it.

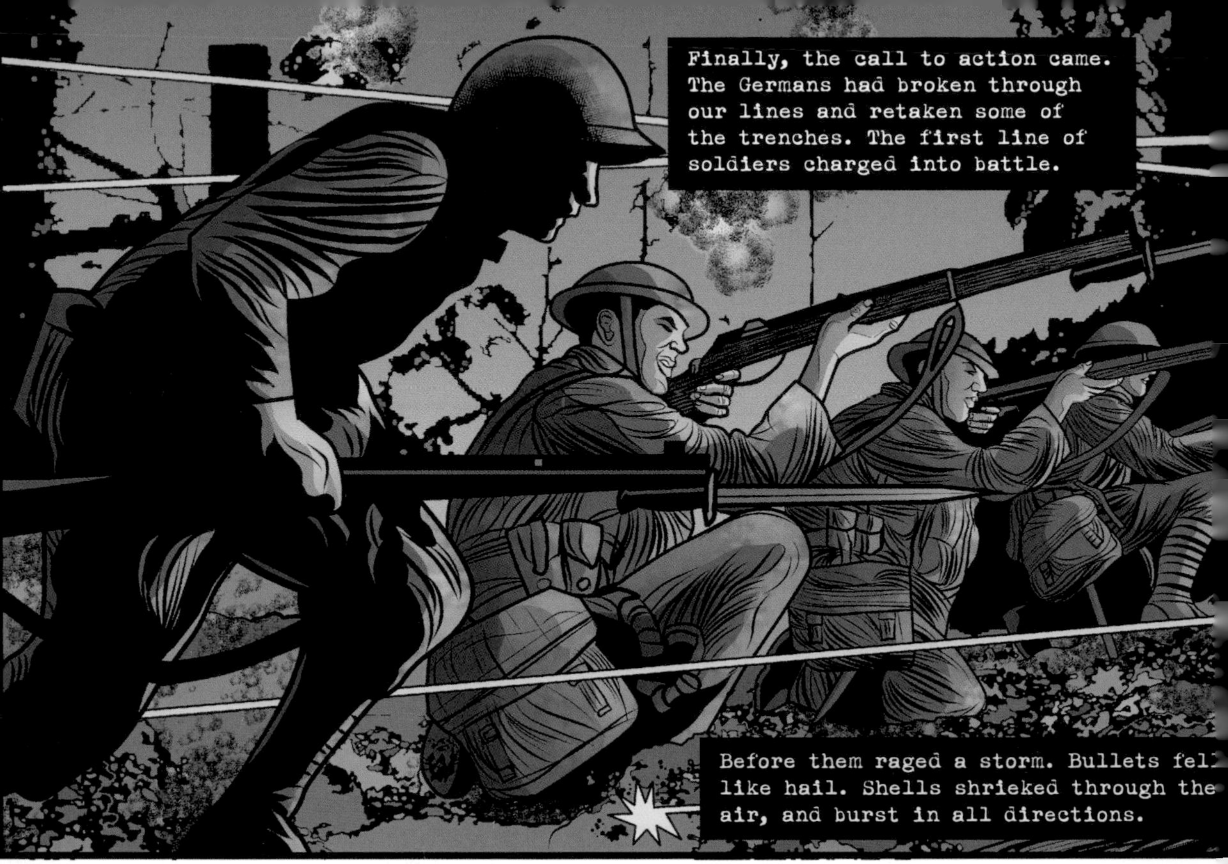
Finally, the call to action came. The Germans had broken through our lines and retaken some of the trenches. The first line of soldiers charged into battle.
Before them raged a storm. Bullets fell like hail. Shells shrieked through the air, and burst in all directions.

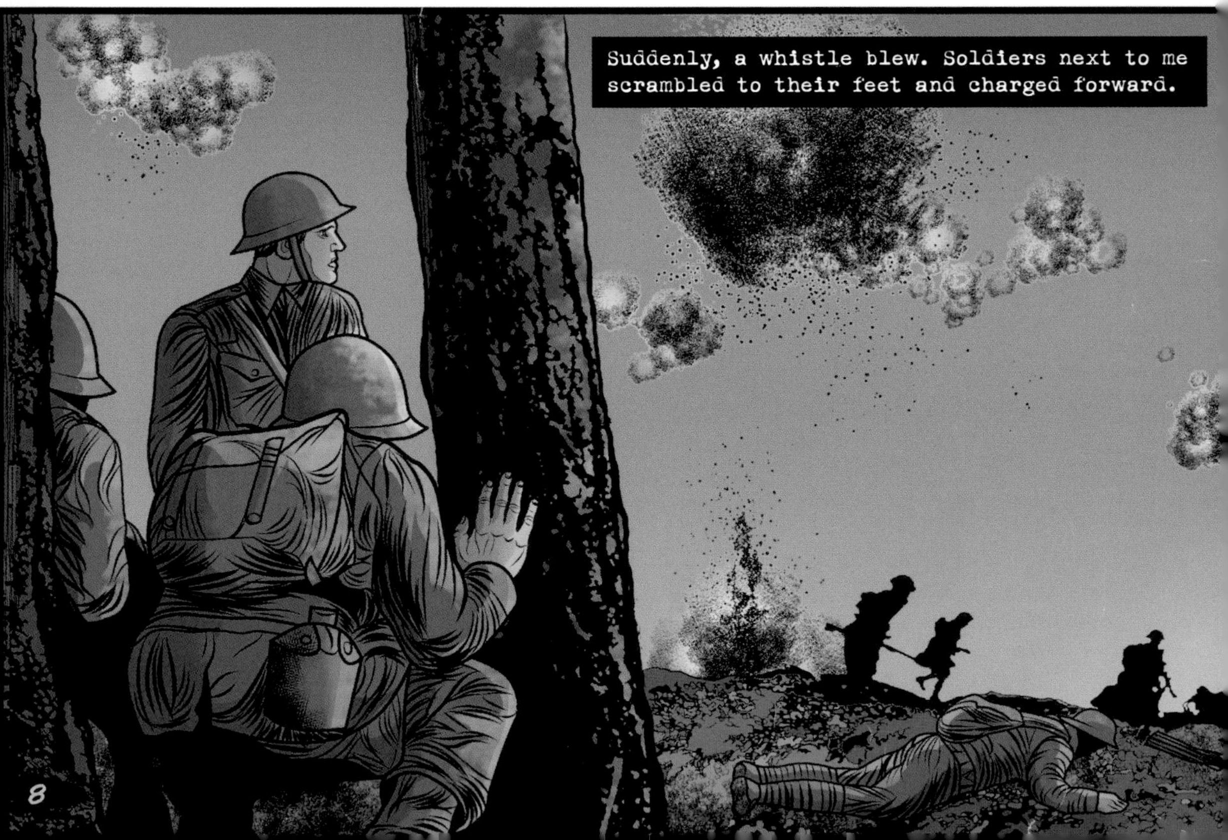
Suddenly, a whistle blew. Soldiers next to me scrambled to their feet and charged forward.

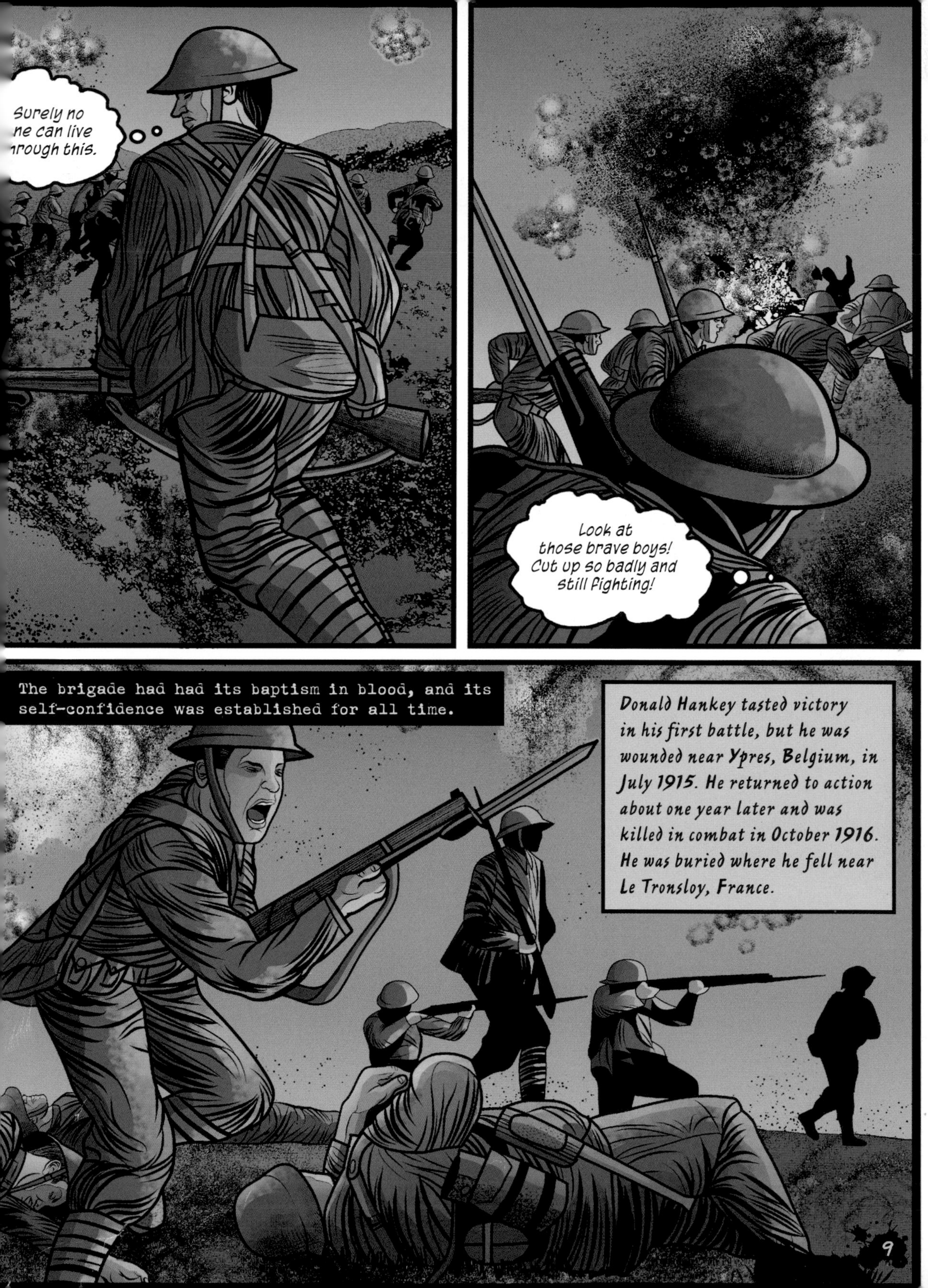
Surely no ne can live hrough this.
Look at those brave boys! Cut up so badly and still fighting!
The brigade had had its baptism in blood, and its self-confidence was established for all time.
Donald Hankey tasted victory in his first battle, but he was wounded near Ypres, Belgium, in July 1915. He returned to action about one year later and was killed in combat in October 1916. He was buried where he fell near Le Tronsloy, France.

CH. 3

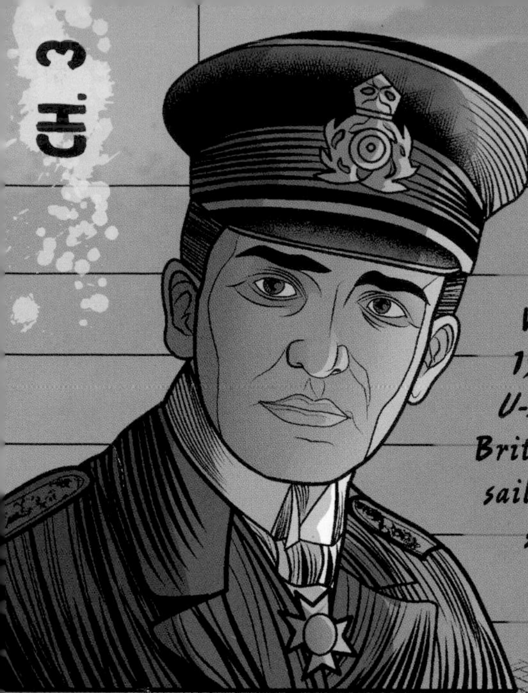

Walther Schwieger: Sinking of the *Lusitania*

Walther Schwieger joined the German marines in 1903. In 1914 he was given command of the deadly U-20 U-boat. On May 7, 1915, Schwieger spotted the British ocean liner RMS *Lusitania*. The *Lusitania* was sailing from New York to Liverpool, England. Schwieger suspected the ship was carrying ammunition and other war supplies for the Allied forces.

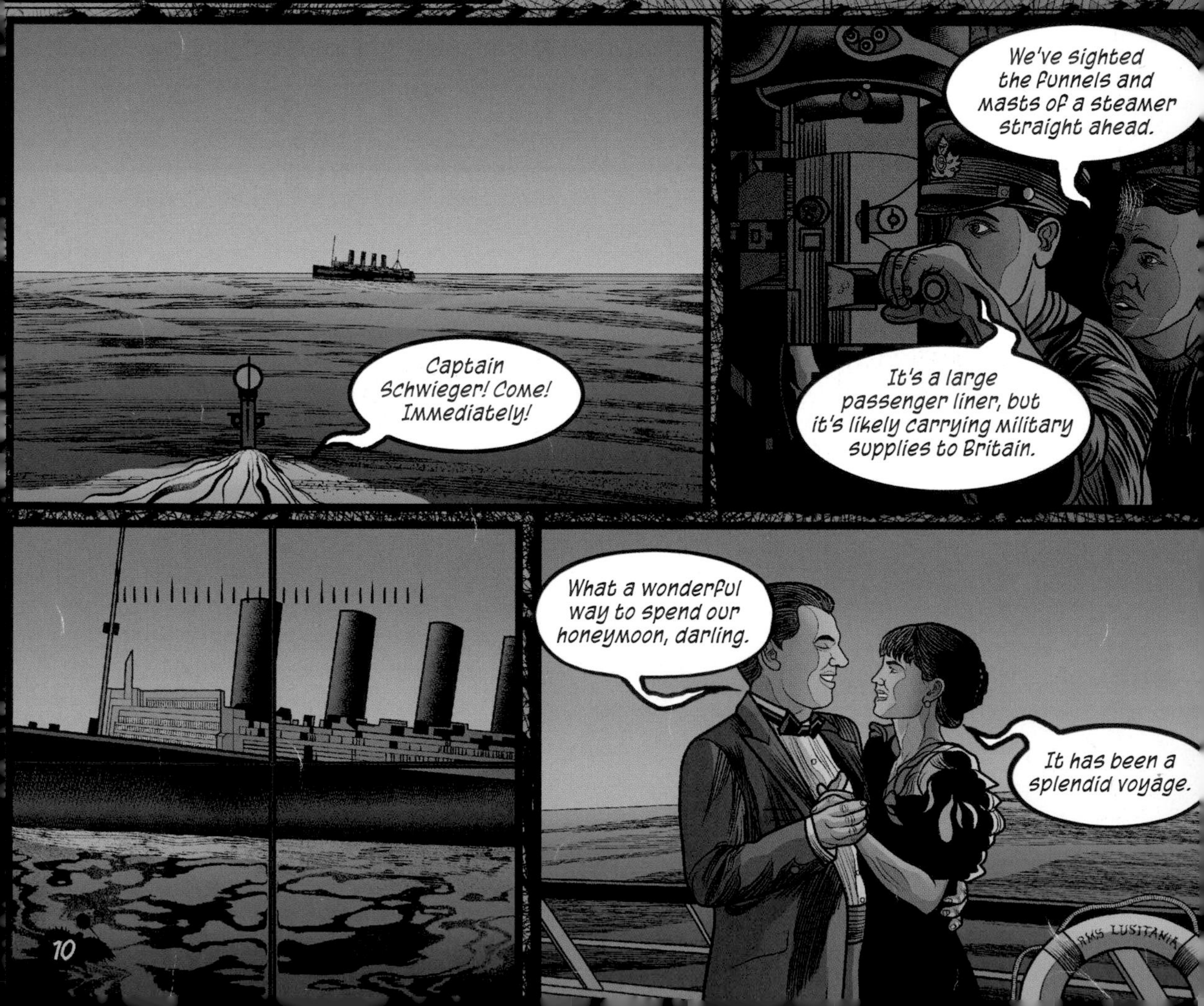

Captain Schwieger! Come! Immediately!
We've sighted the funnels and masts of a steamer straight ahead.
It's a large passenger liner, but it's likely carrying military supplies to Britain.
What a wonderful way to spend our honeymoon, darling.
It has been a splendid voyage.
RMS LUSITANIA

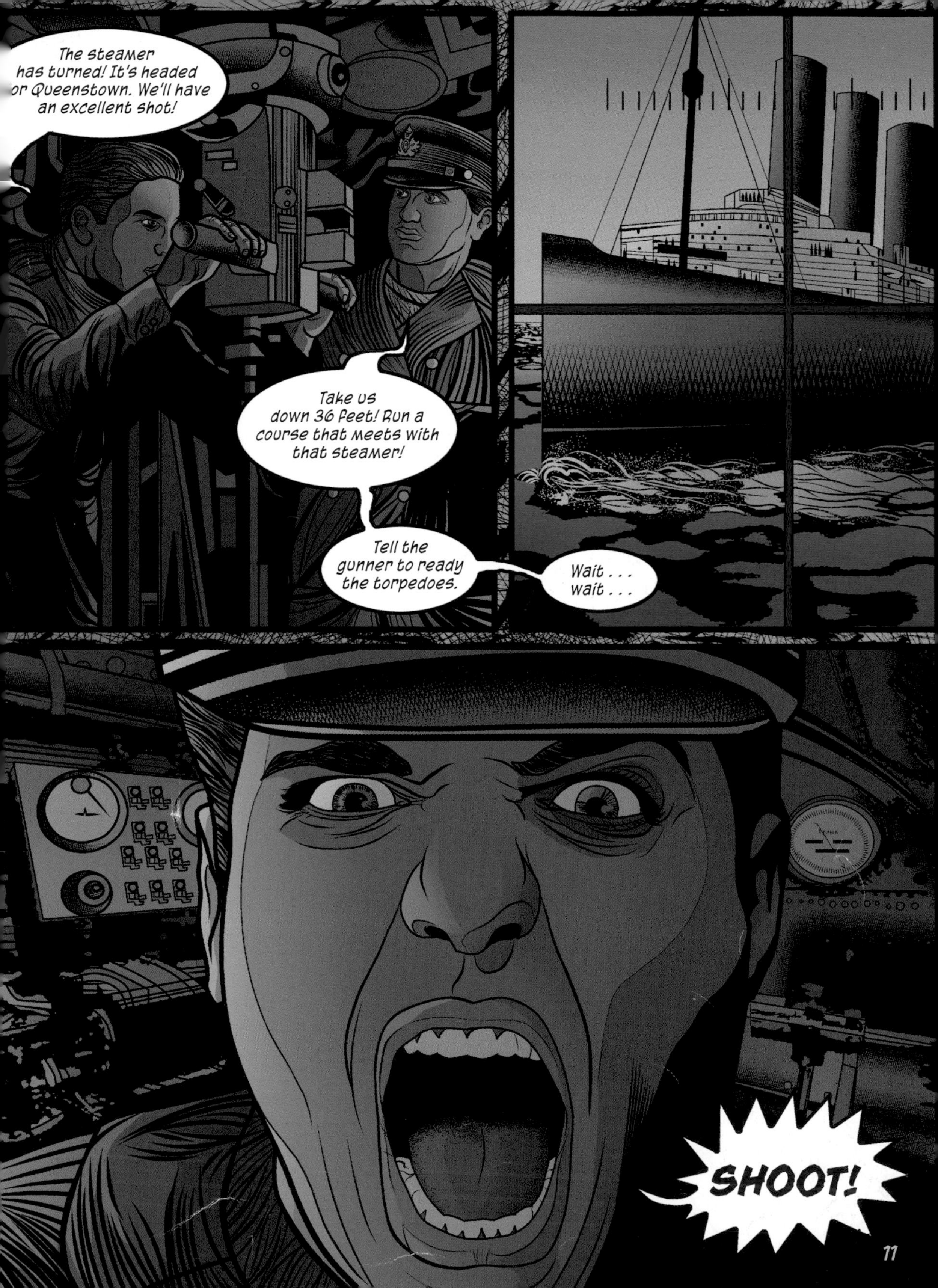
The steamer has turned! It's headed or Queenstown. We'll have an excellent shot!
Take us down 36 feet! Run a course that meets with that steamer!
Tell the gunner to ready the torpedoes.
Wait . . . wait . . .
SHOOT!

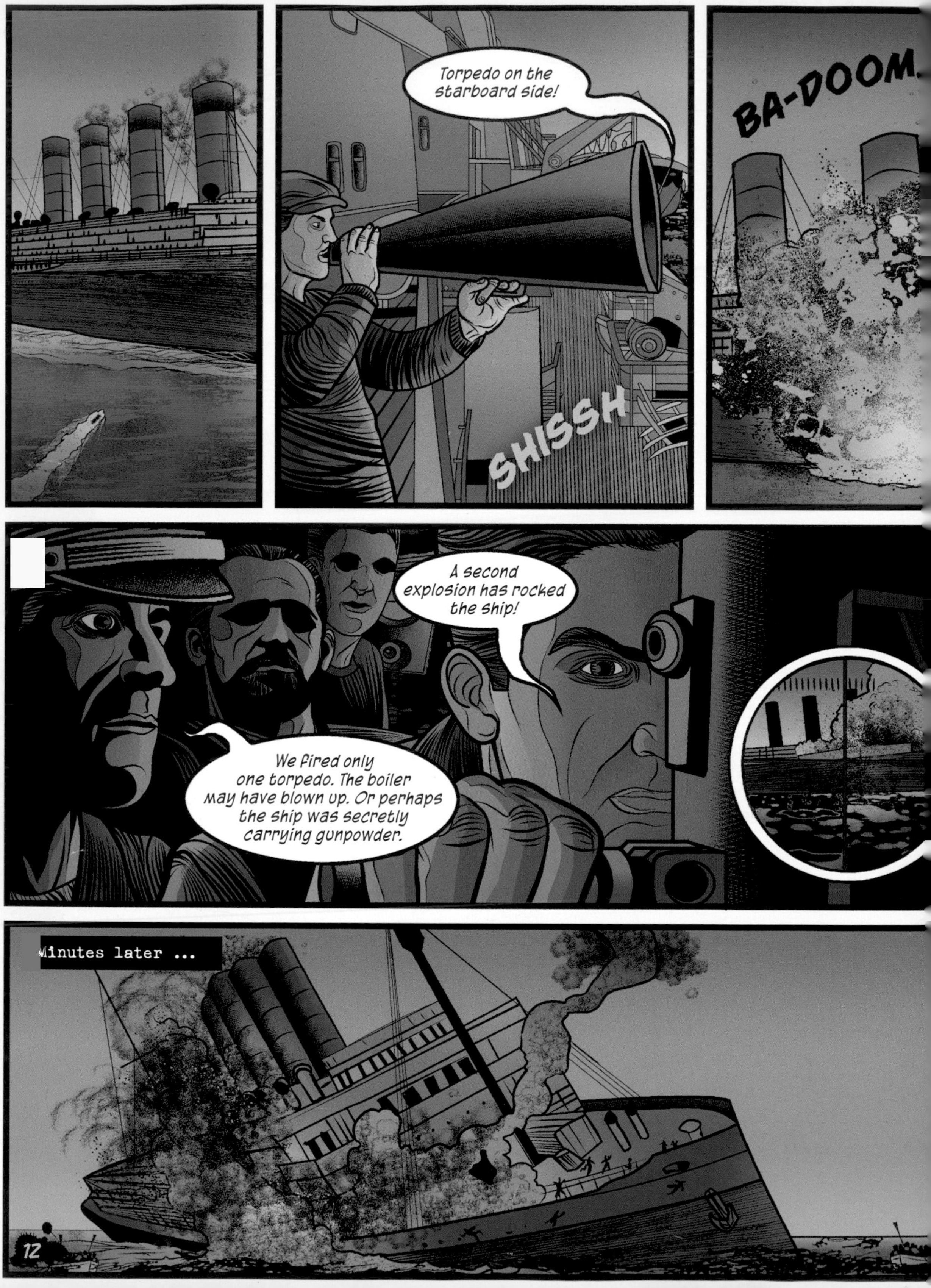
Torpedo on the starboard side!
SHISSH
BA-DOOM
A second explosion has rocked the ship!
We fired only one torpedo. The boiler may have blown up. Or perhaps the ship was secretly carrying gunpowder.
Minutes later ...

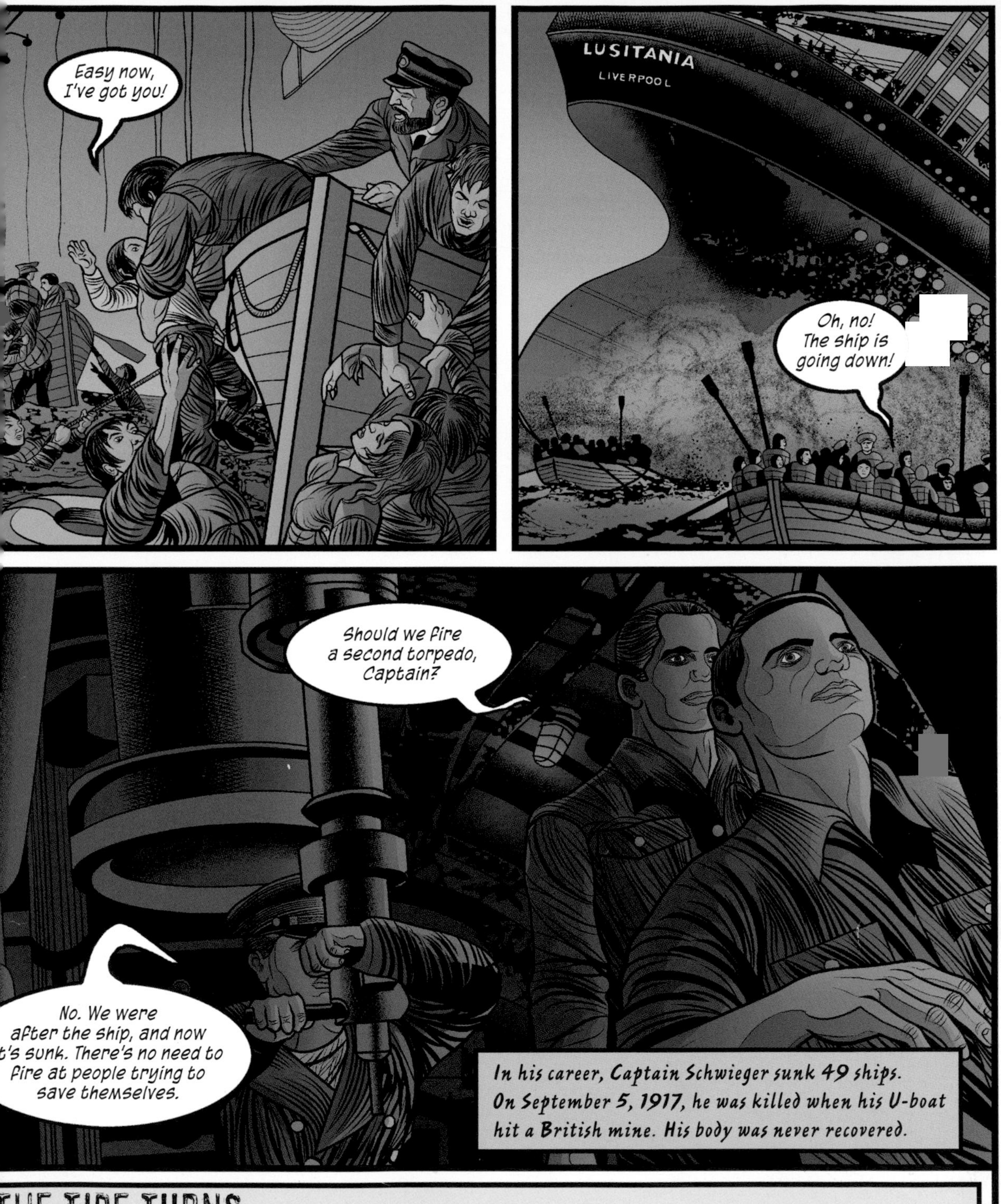
Easy now, I've got you!
LUSITANIA
LIVERPOOL
Oh, no! The ship is going down!
Should we fire a second torpedo, Captain?
No. We were after the ship, and now t's sunk. There's no need to fire at people trying to save themselves.
In his career, Captain Schwieger sunk 49 ships. On September 5, 1917, he was killed when his U-boat hit a British mine. His body was never recovered.

THE TIDE TURNS

The sinking of the Lusitania had a huge impact on the direction of World War I. At the time of its sinking, the United States was not yet fighting in the war. But the death of 1,198 people on an unarmed passenger ship outraged many Americans. The event turned public opinion against Germany. It fueled the United States' entrance into the war in 1917.

CH. 4

Alan Seeger: Rendezvous with Death

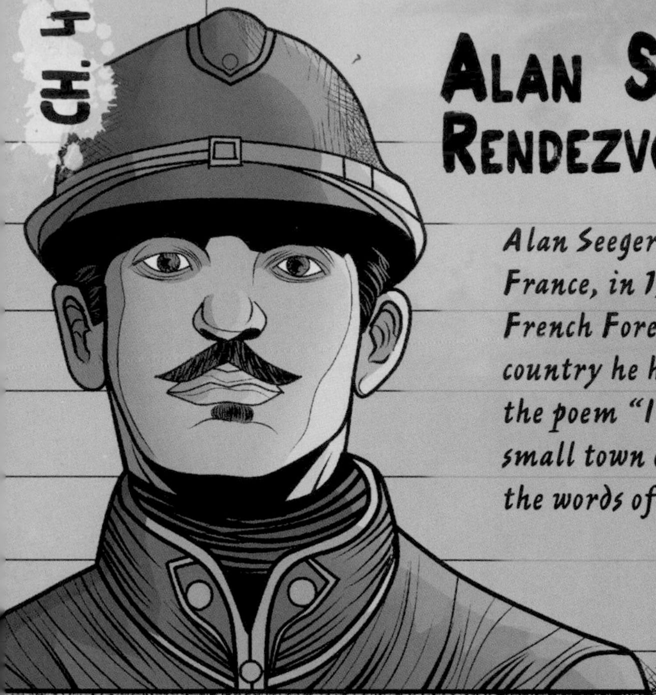

Alan Seeger was an American poet who moved to Paris, France, in 1914. When war broke out, he joined the French Foreign Legion. He wanted to fight for the country he had come to love. During the war, Seeger wrote the poem "I Have a Rendezvous with Death." Outside the small town of Belloy-en-Santerre in northern France, the words of this poem echoed his destiny.

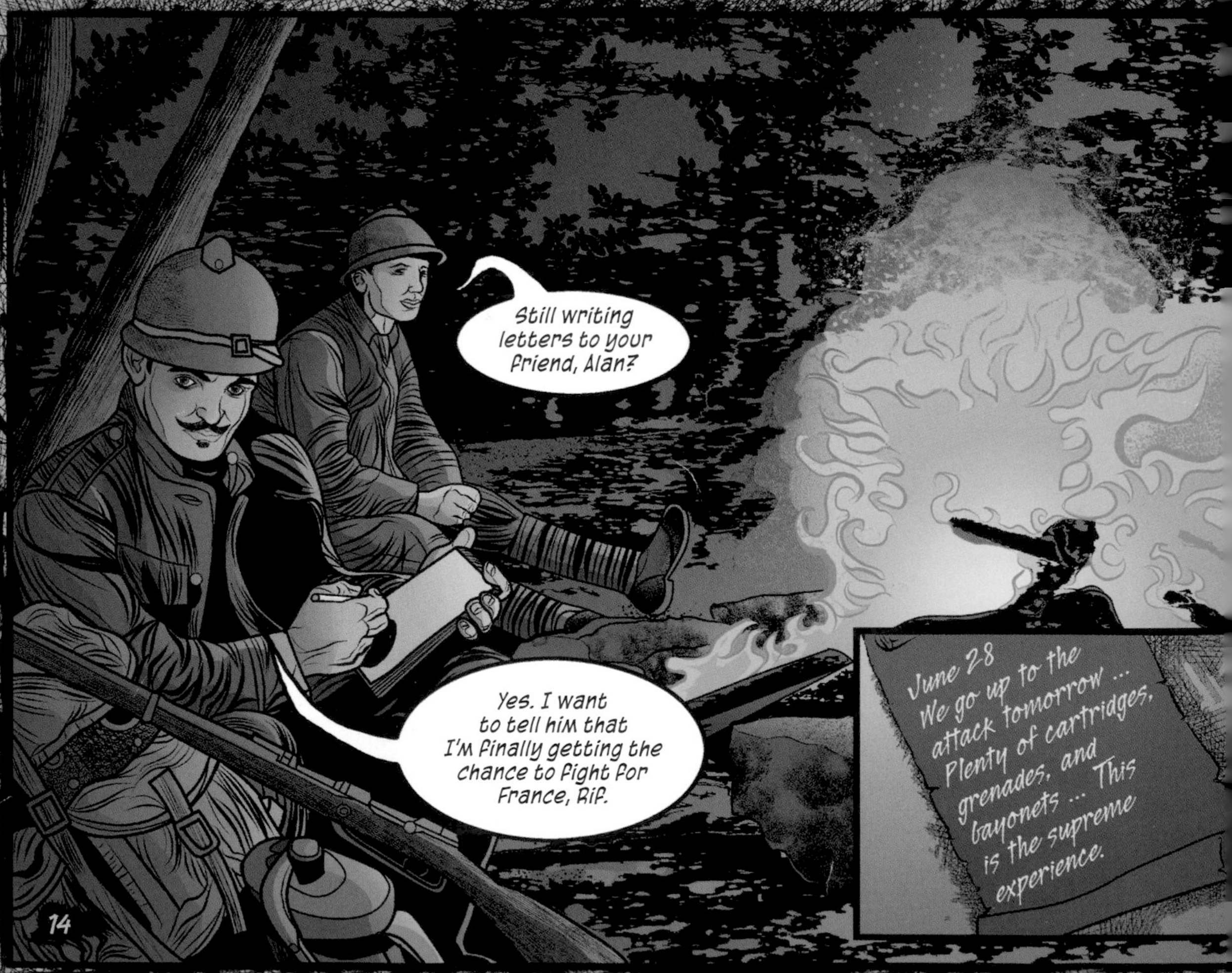
Still writing letters to your friend, Alan?
Yes. I want to tell him that I'm finally getting the chance to fight for France, Rif.
June 28
We go up to the attack tomorrow ... Plenty of cartridges, grenades, and bayonets ... This is the supreme experience.

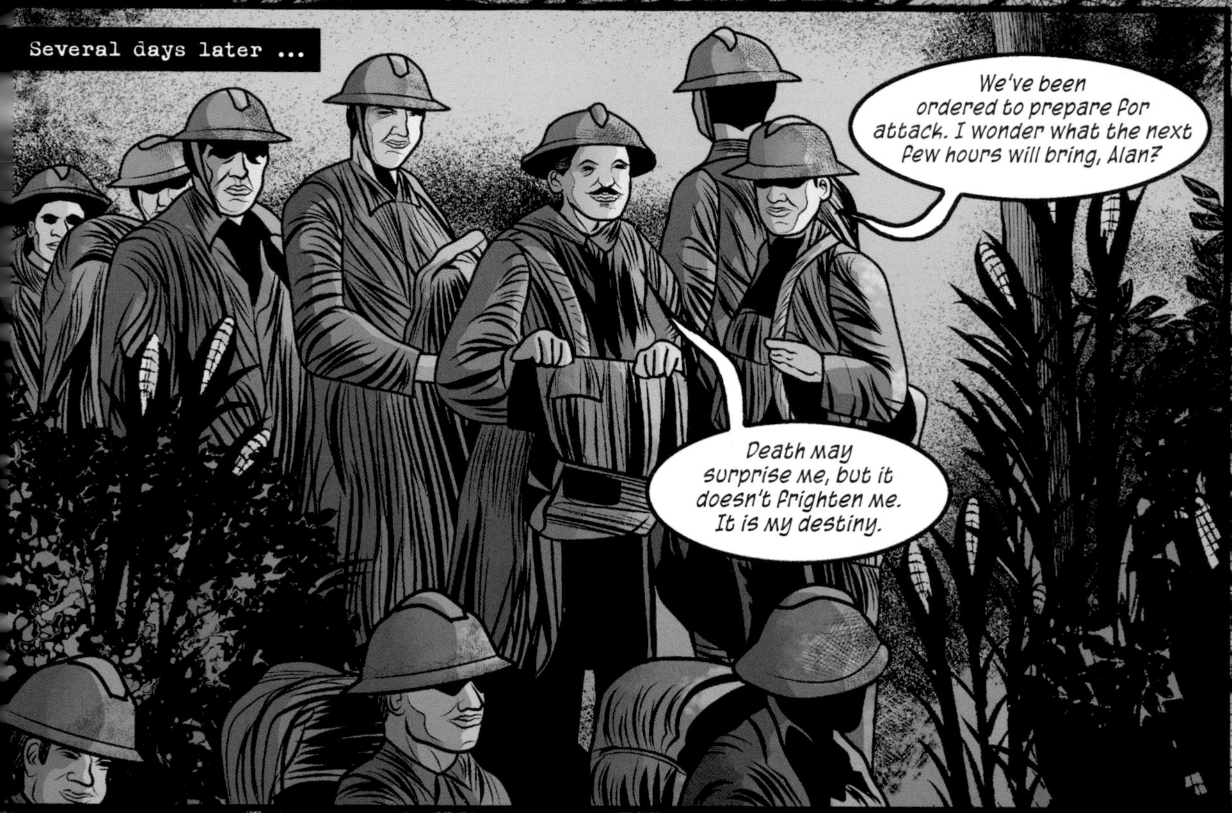
Several days later ...
We've been ordered to prepare for attack. I wonder what the next few hours will bring, Alan?
Death may surprise me, but it doesn't frighten me. It is my destiny.

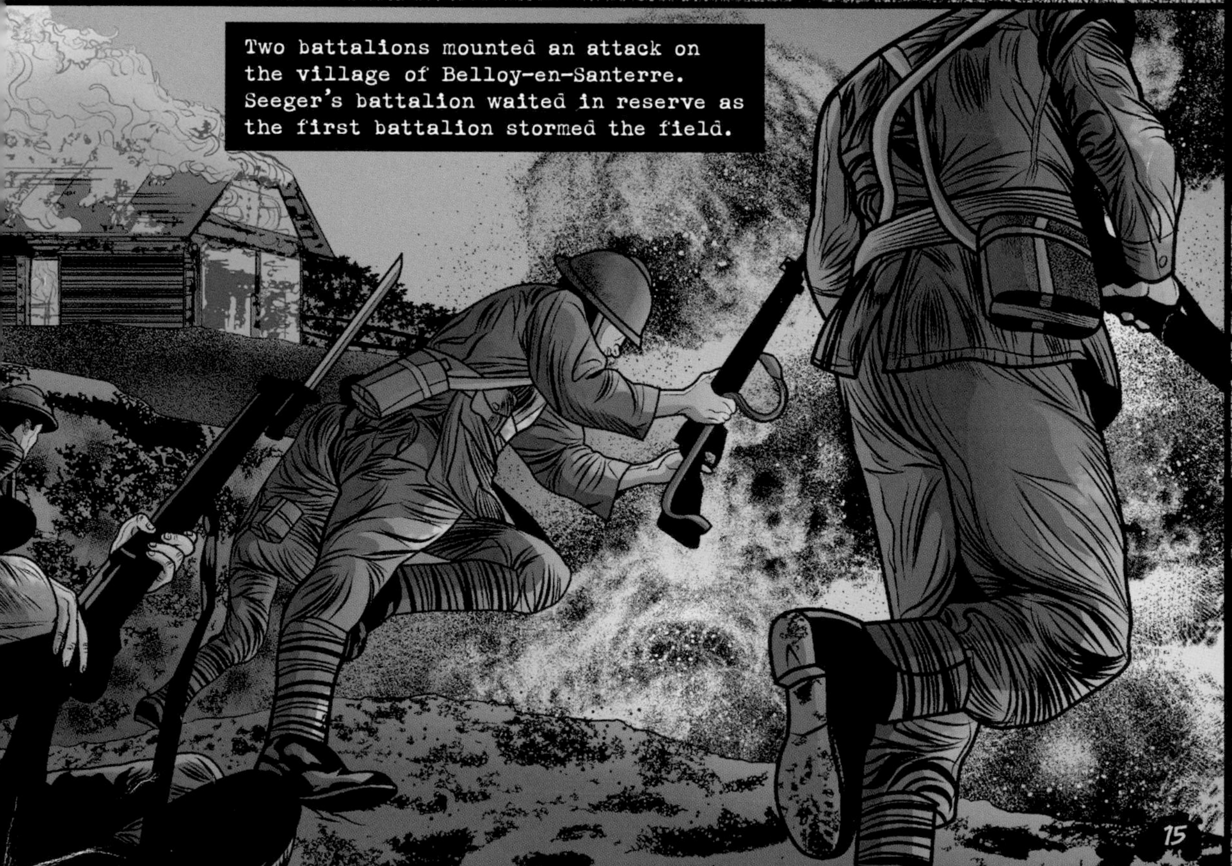
Two battalions mounted an attack on the village of Belloy-en-Santerre. Seeger's battalion waited in reserve as the first battalion stormed the field.

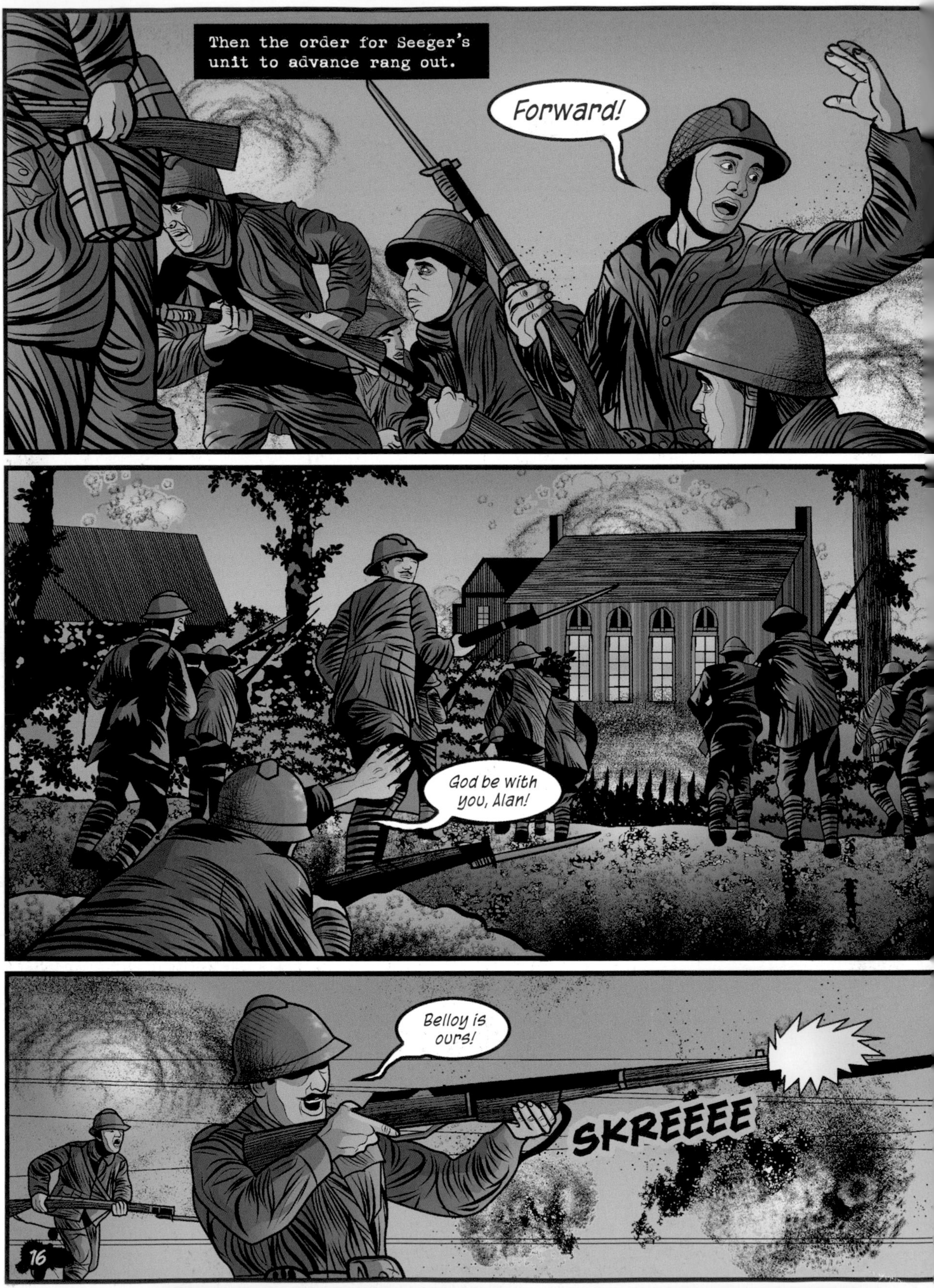

Then the order for Seeger's unit to advance rang out.
Forward!
God be with you, Alan!
Belloy is ours!
SKREEEE

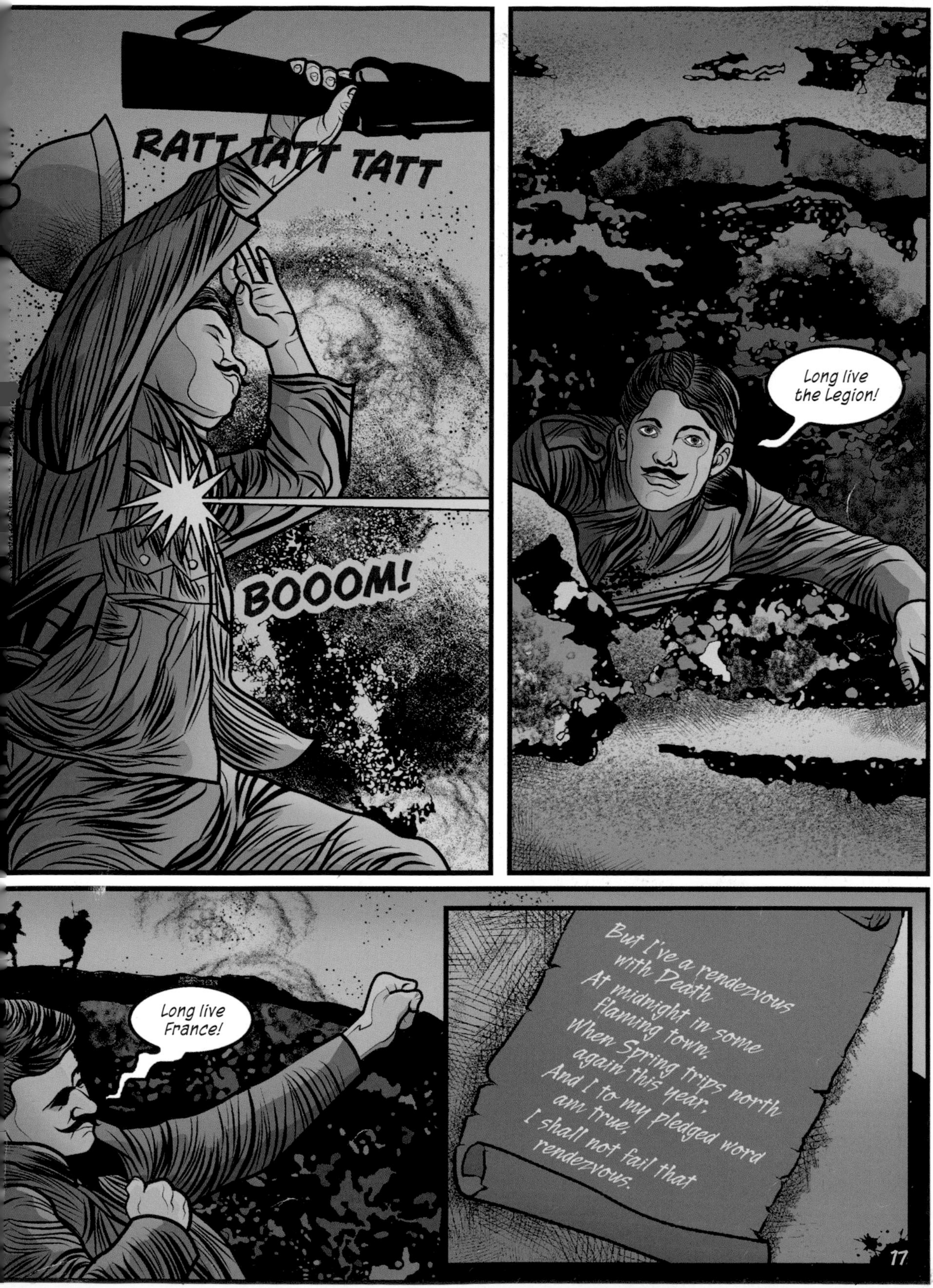
RATT TATT TATT
BOOOM!
Long live the Legion!
Long live France!
But I've a rendezvous with Death
At midnight in some flaming town,
When Spring trips north again this year,
And I to my pledged word am true,
I shall not fail that rendezvous.

CH. 5

Alvin York: American Hero

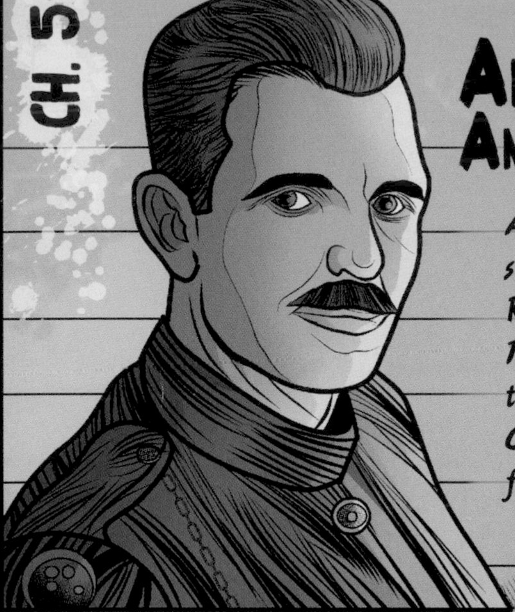

Alvin York was born in Tennessee in 1887. He served as corporal in Company G, 328th Infantry Regiment, 82nd Infantry Division. On October 8, 1918, York's battalion was ordered to drive German troops from their positions along a railroad line near Chatel-Chéhéry in northern France. In the hours that followed, York became a one-man "war machine."

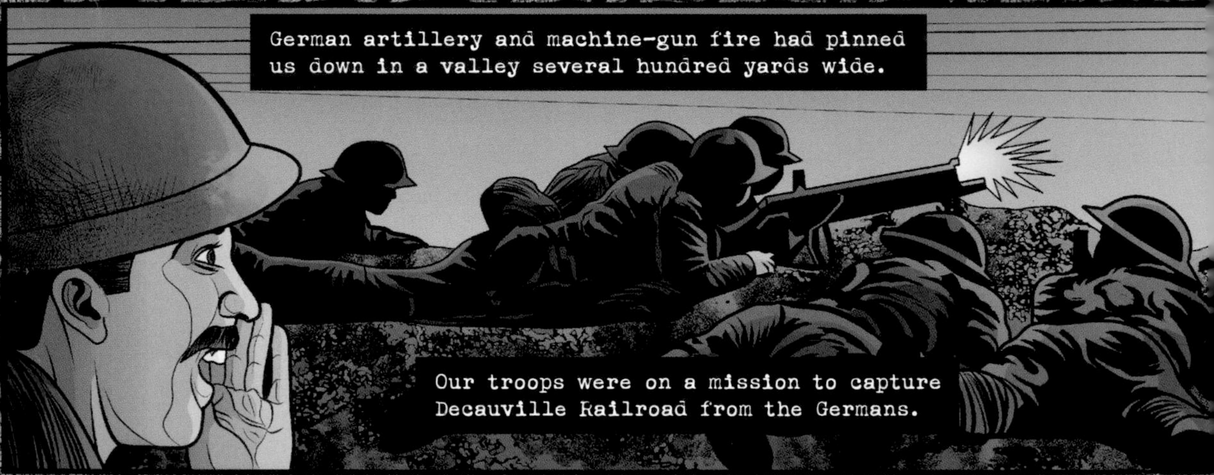
German artillery and machine-gun fire had pinned us down in a valley several hundred yards wide.
Our troops were on a mission to capture Decauville Railroad from the Germans.

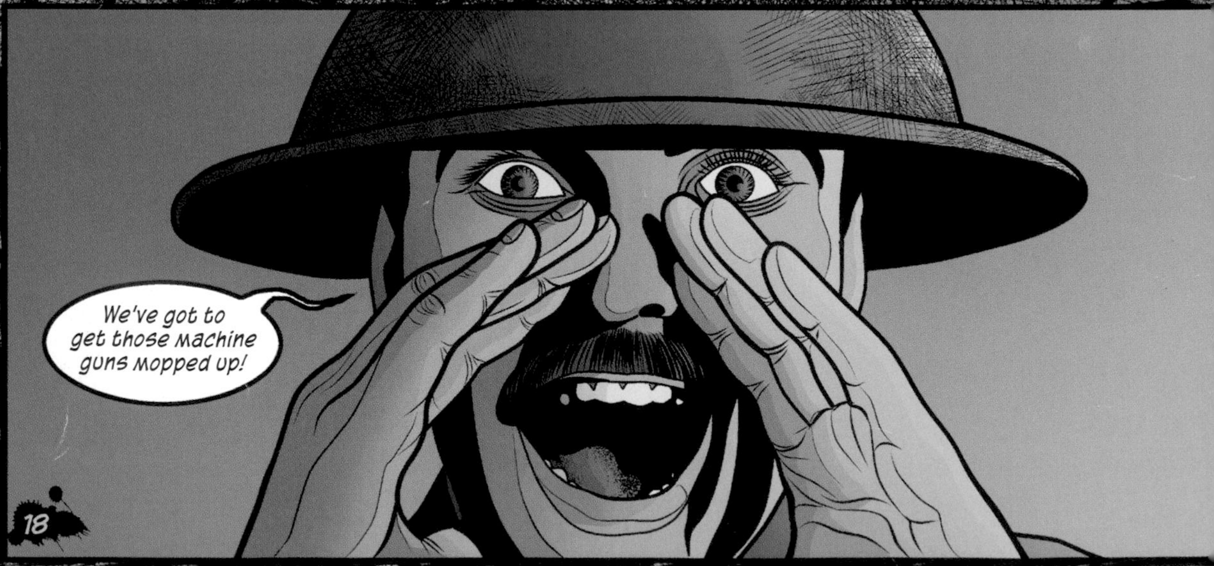
We've got to get those machine guns mopped up!

More than 30 machine guns were hidden in the ridges 300 yards away. A small group of us decided to surprise them by sneaking behind their lines and attacking from the rear.

It'll be 17 of us against all them Germans, boys! Let's make every shot count!

We dashed from bush to bush until we came up behind enemy lines.

We'd found their camp headquarters. They must have thought the whole American army was behind them.

Comrade! Don't shoot!

We won't, major. Take these prisoners away.

19

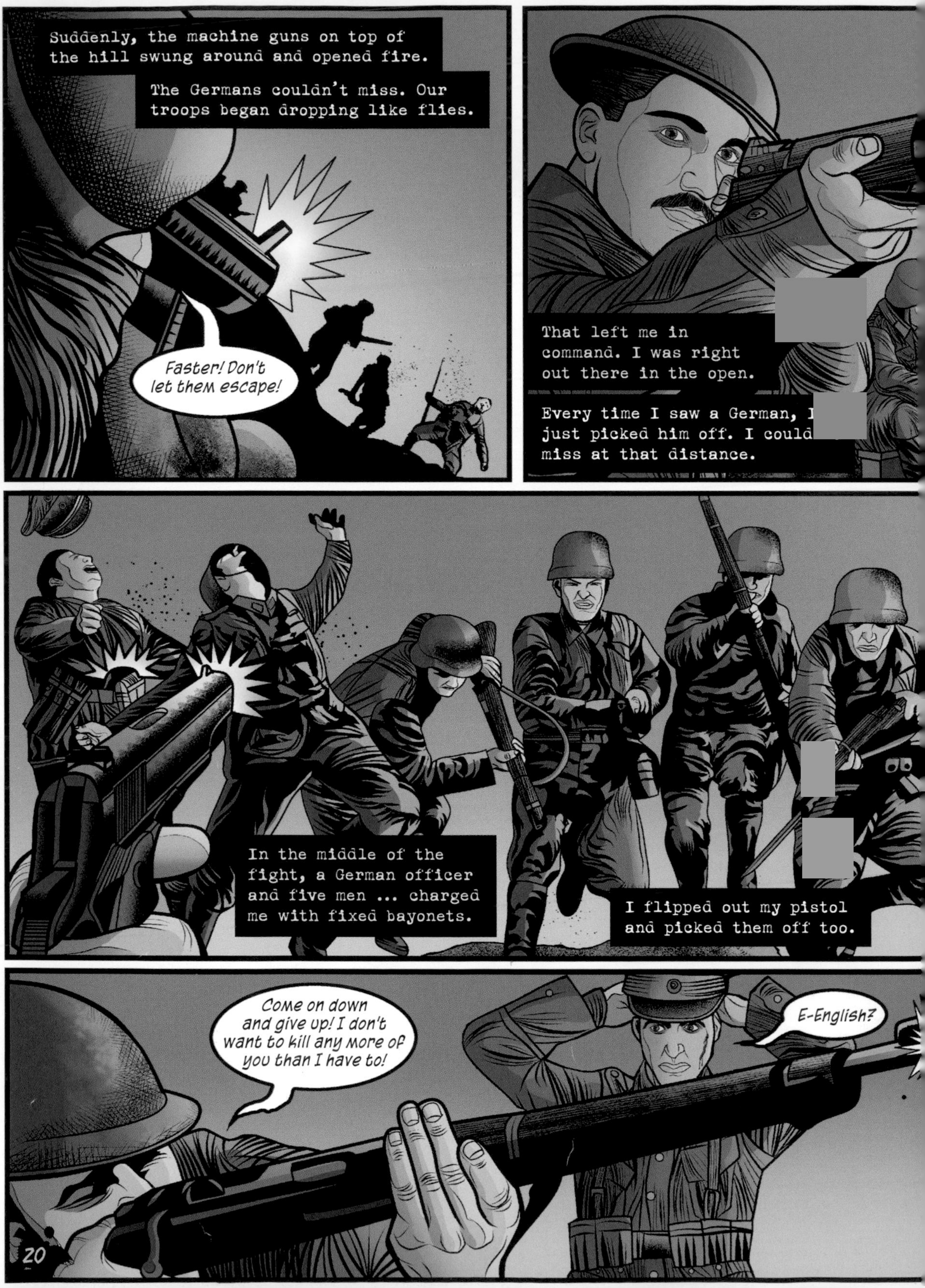

Suddenly, the machine guns on top of the hill swung around and opened fire.
The Germans couldn't miss. Our troops began dropping like flies.
Faster! Don't let them escape!
That left me in command. I was right out there in the open.
Every time I saw a German, I just picked him off. I could
miss at that distance.
In the middle of the fight, a German officer and five men ... charged me with fixed bayonets.
I flipped out my pistol and picked them off too.
Come on down and give up! I don't want to kill any more of you than I have to!
E-English?

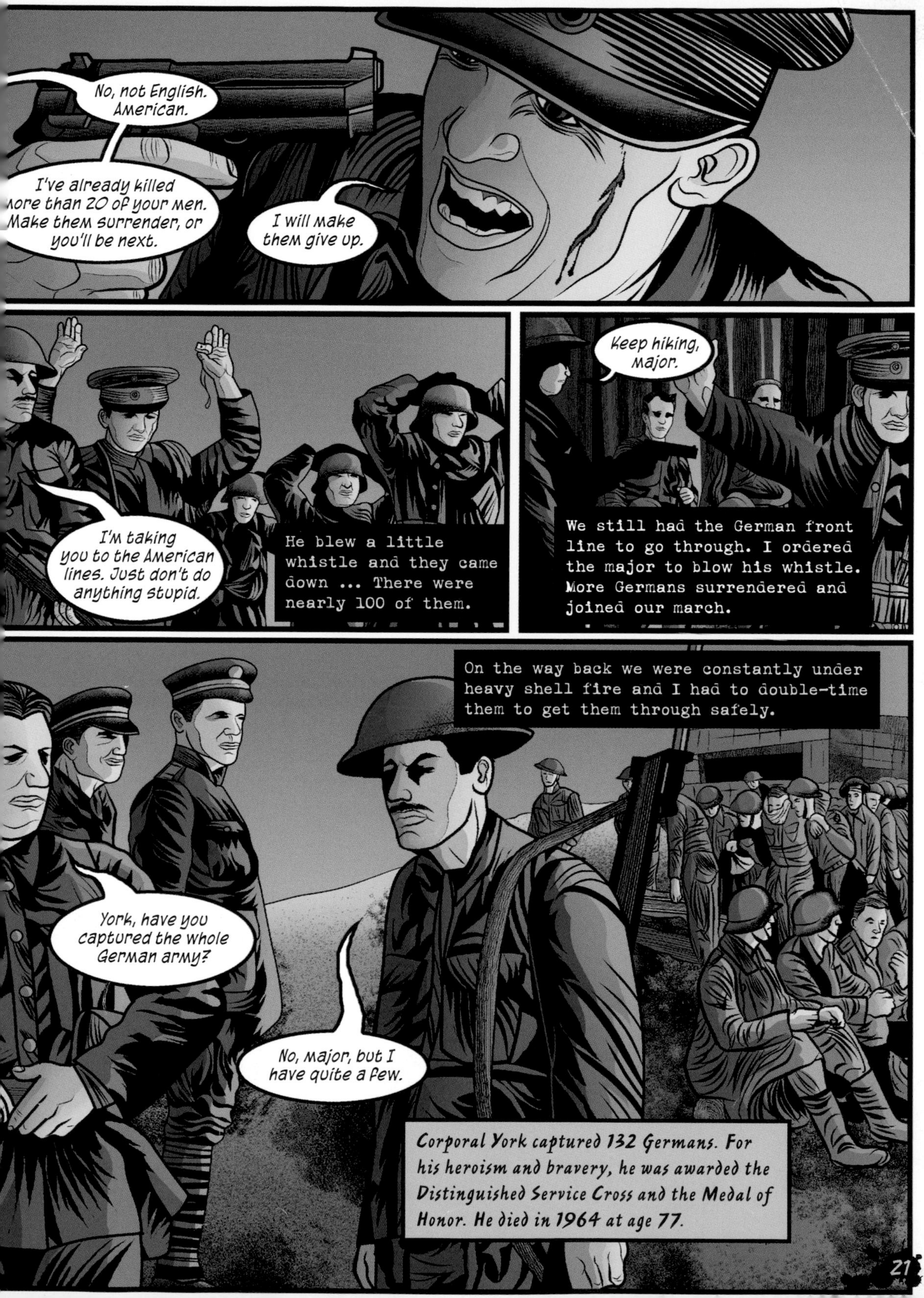
No, not English. American.
I've already killed more than 20 of your men. Make them surrender, or you'll be next.
I will make them give up.
I'm taking you to the American lines. Just don't do anything stupid.
He blew a little whistle and they came down ... There were nearly 100 of them.
Keep hiking, major.
We still had the German front line to go through. I ordered the major to blow his whistle. More Germans surrendered and joined our march.
On the way back we were constantly under heavy shell fire and I had to double-time them to get them through safely.
York, have you captured the whole German army?
No, major, but I have quite a few.
Corporal York captured 132 Germans. For his heroism and bravery, he was awarded the Distinguished Service Cross and the Medal of Honor. He died in 1964 at age 77.

CH. 6

Baron Manfred Albrecht von Richthofen: The Red Baron

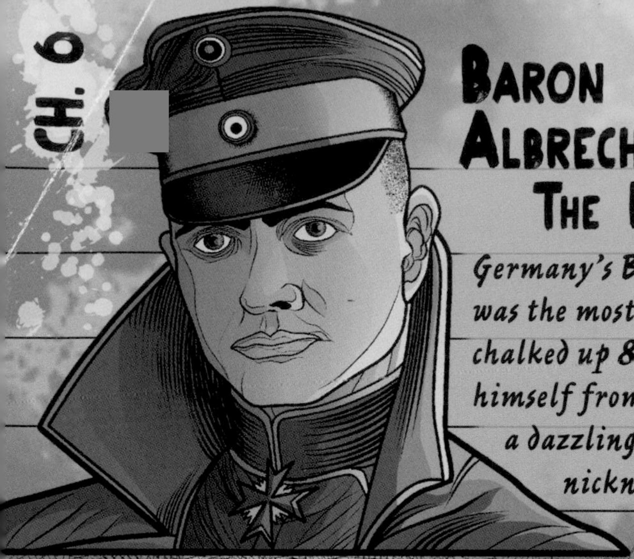

Germany's Baron Manfred Albrecht von Richthofen was the most famous flying ace of World War I. He chalked up 80 combat kills during the war. To distinguish himself from other pilots, Richthofen painted his planes a dazzling red. His blazing red planes earned him the nickname the "Red Baron."

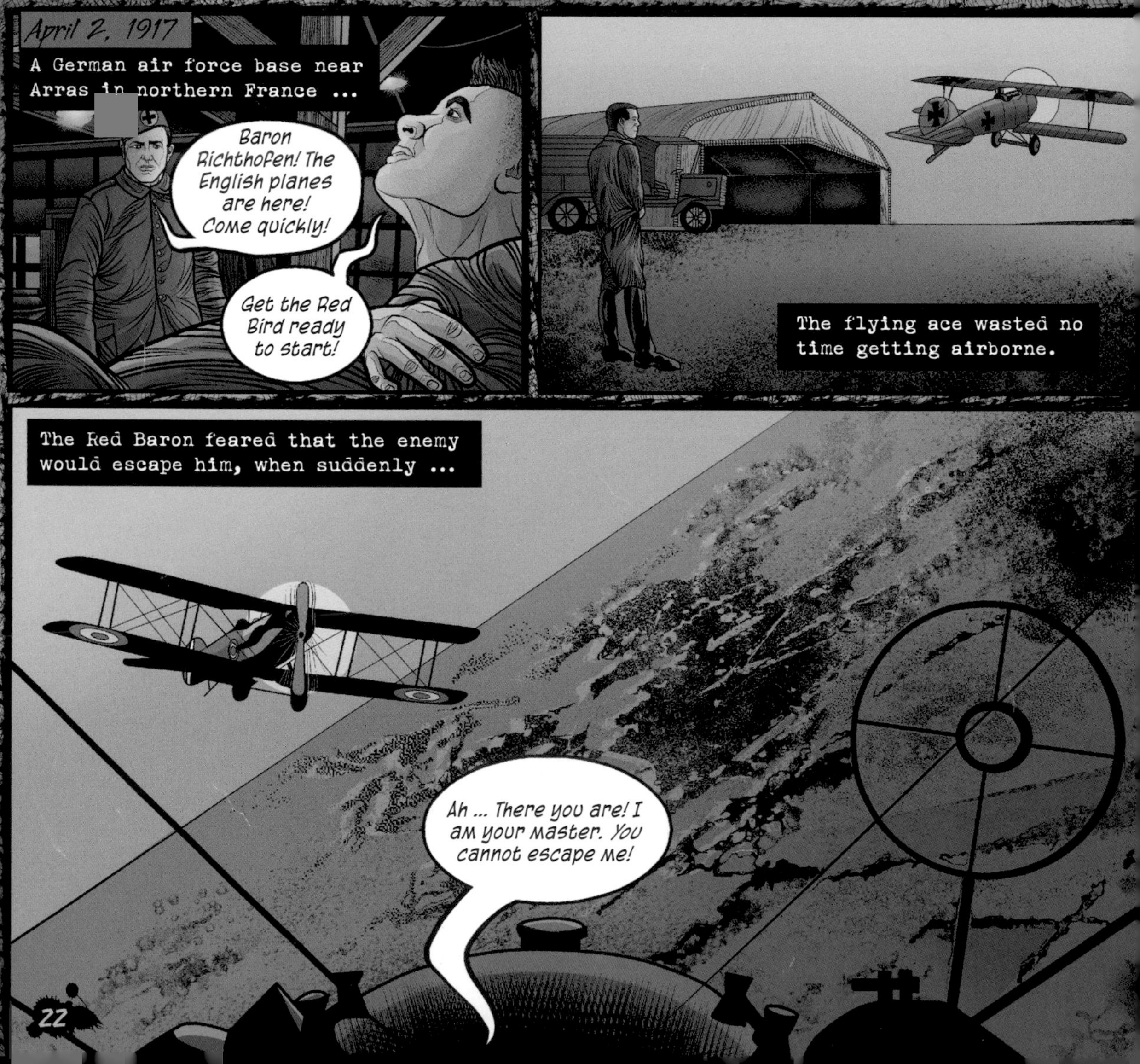

April 2, 1917
A German air force base near Arras in northern France ...
Baron Richthofen! The English planes are here! Come quickly!
Get the Red Bird ready to start!
The flying ace wasted no time getting airborne.
The Red Baron feared that the enemy would escape him, when suddenly ...
Ah ... There you are! I am your master. You cannot escape me!

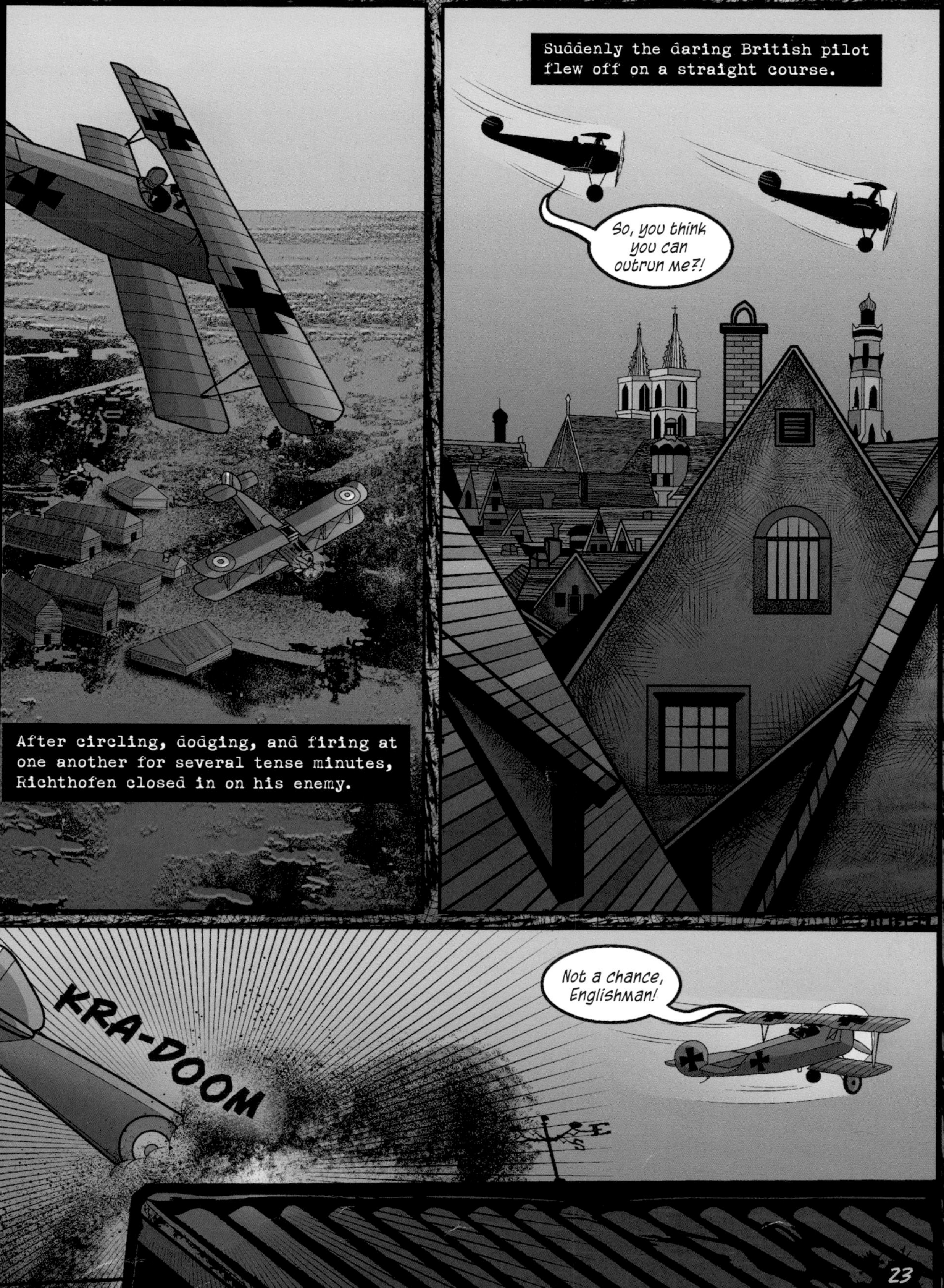
After circling, dodging, and firing at one another for several tense minutes, Richthofen closed in on his enemy.
Suddenly the daring British pilot flew off on a straight course.
So, you think you can outrun me?!
KRA-DOOM
Not a chance, Englishman!

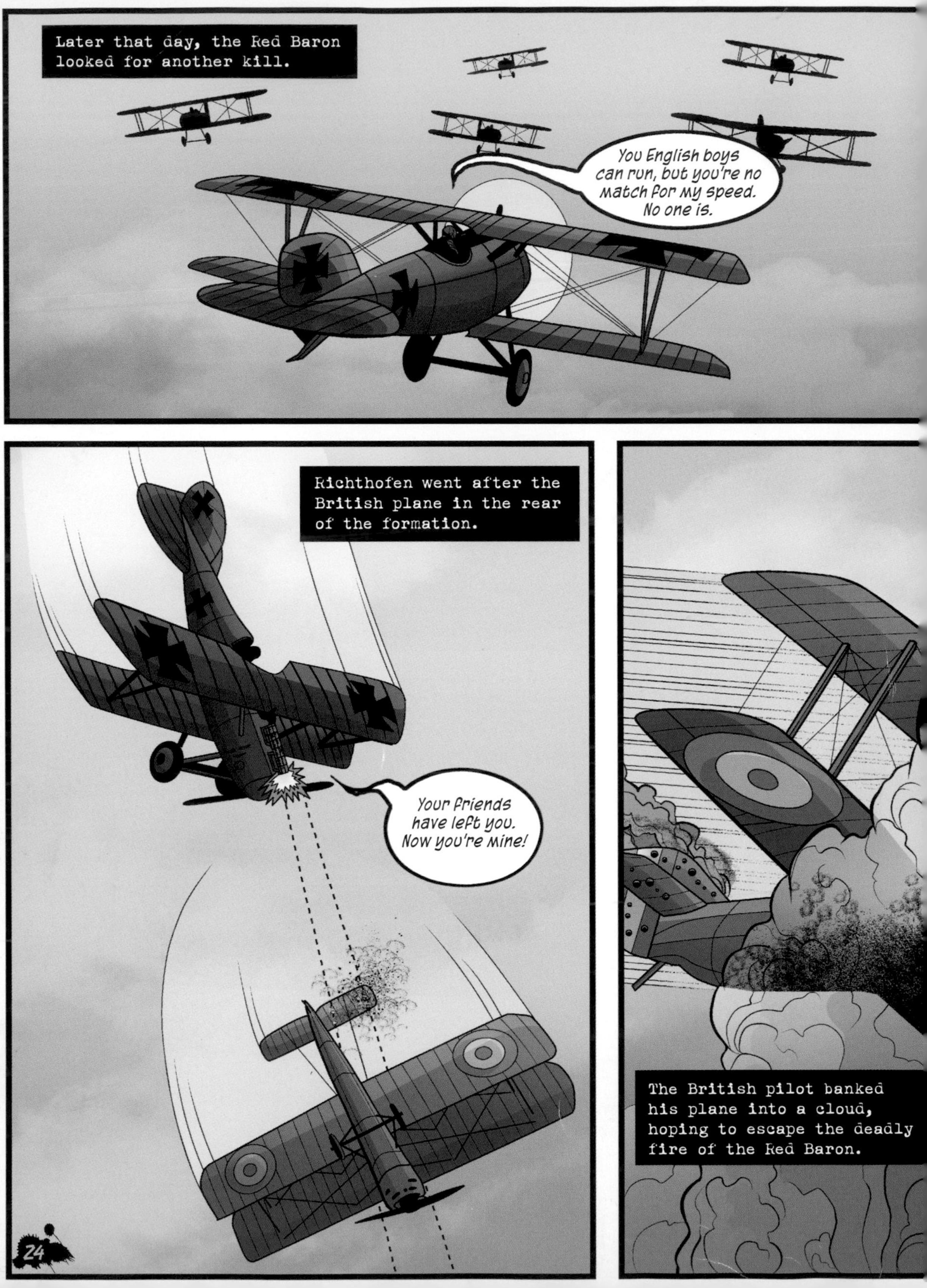
Later that day, the Red Baron looked for another kill.
You English boys can run, but you're no match for my speed. No one is.
Richthofen went after the British plane in the rear of the formation.
Your friends have left you. Now you're mine!
The British pilot banked his plane into a cloud, hoping to escape the deadly fire of the Red Baron.

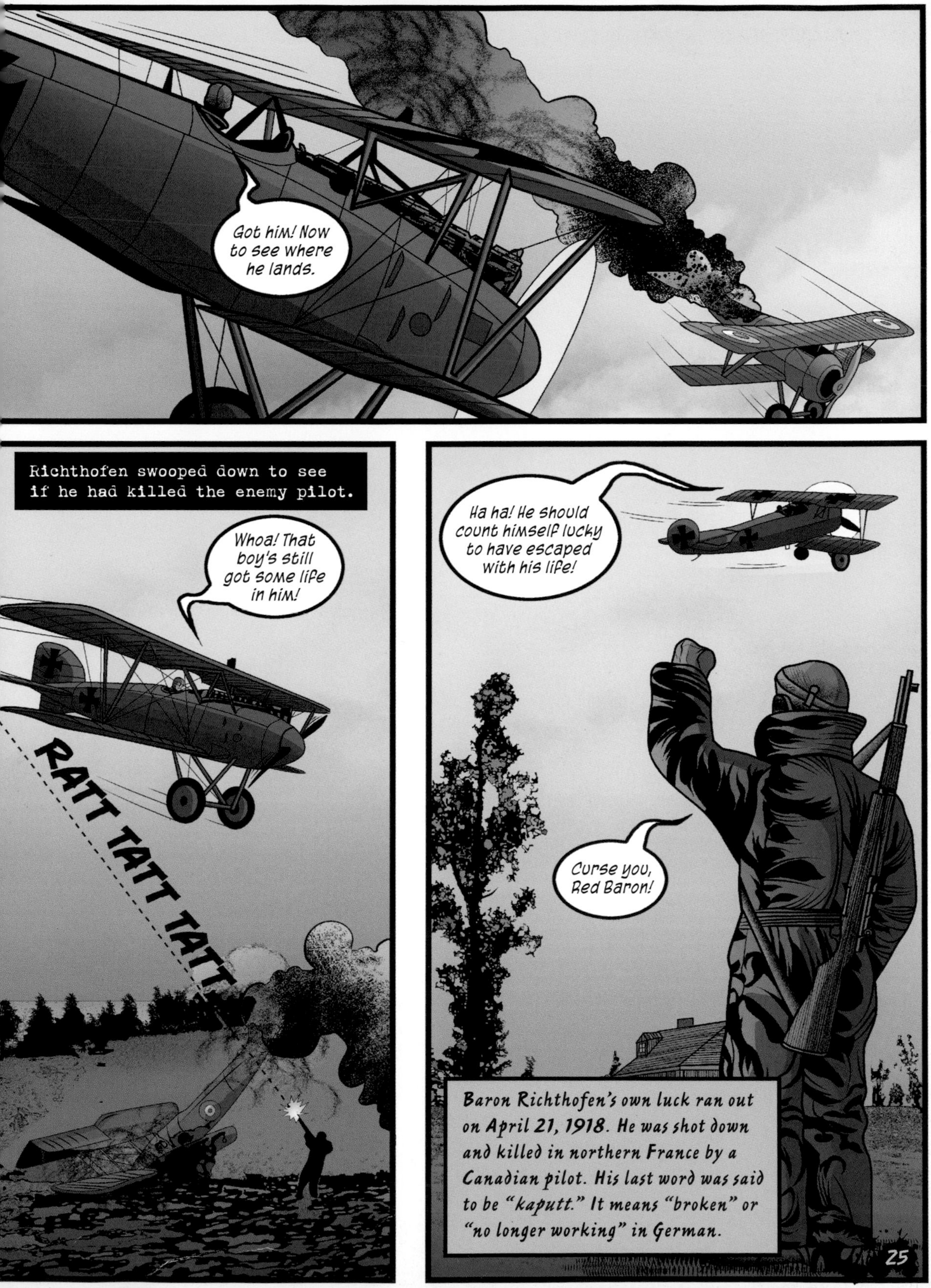
Got him! Now to see where he lands.
Richthofen swooped down to see if he had killed the enemy pilot.
Whoa! That boy's still got some life in him!
RATT TATT TATT
Ha ha! He should count himself lucky to have escaped with his life!
Curse you, Red Baron!
Baron Richthofen's own luck ran out on April 21, 1918. He was shot down and killed in northern France by a Canadian pilot. His last word was said to be "kaputt." It means "broken" or "no longer working" in German.

CH. 7

Arthur Empey: Gas Attack!

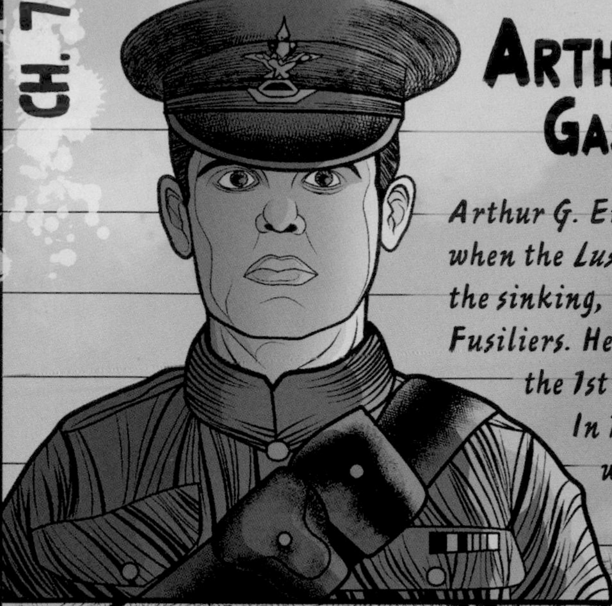

Arthur G. Empey was a sergeant in the U.S. Cavalry when the Lusitania was sunk in May 1915. Angered by the sinking, he traveled to England and joined the Royal Fusiliers. He served with the machine gun company of the 1st Battalion London 56th Infantry Division. In 1916 he experienced the horrors of gas warfare in the trenches of France.

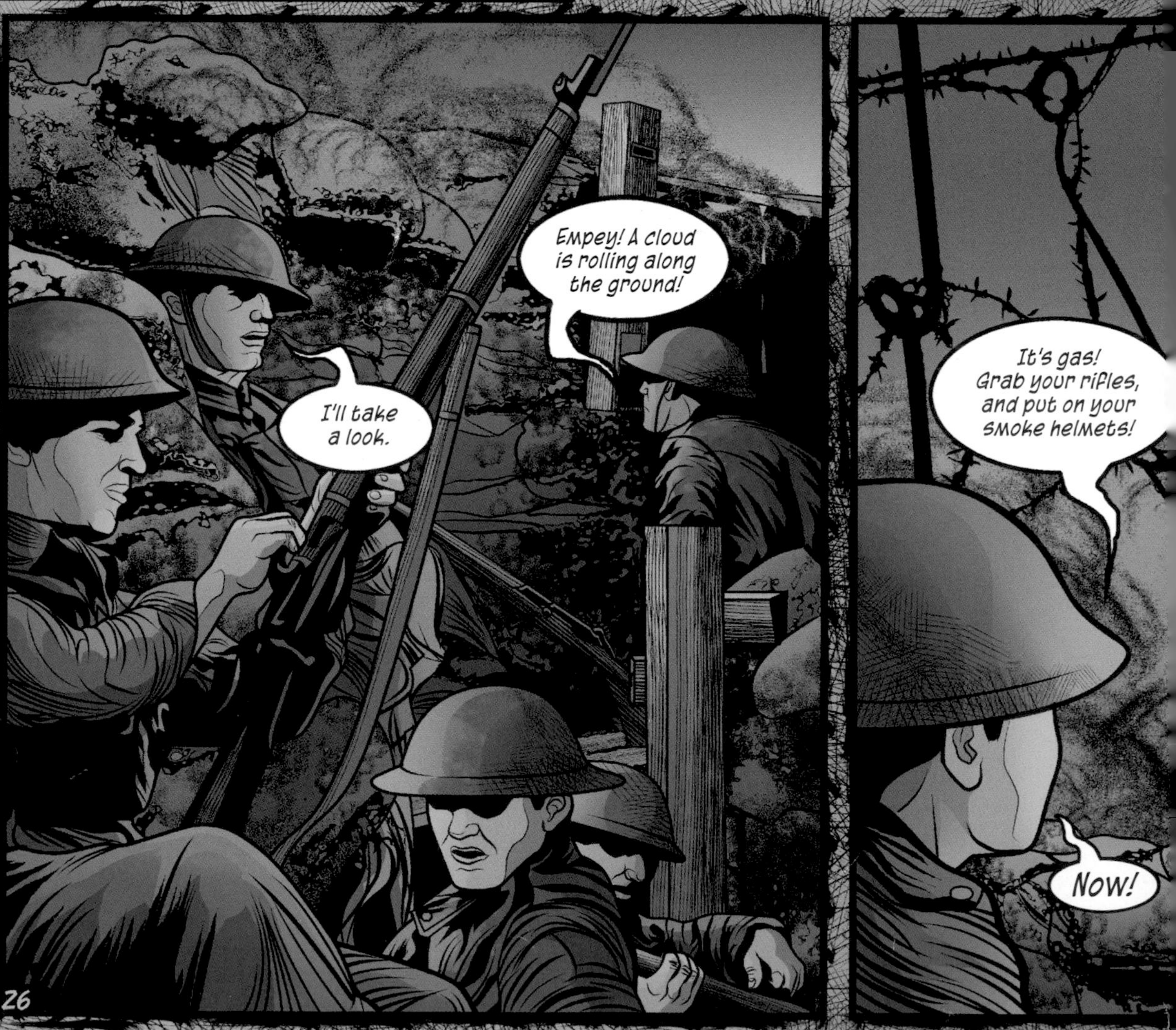
Empey! A cloud is rolling along the ground!
I'll take a look.
It's gas! Grab your rifles, and put on your smoke helmets!
NOW!

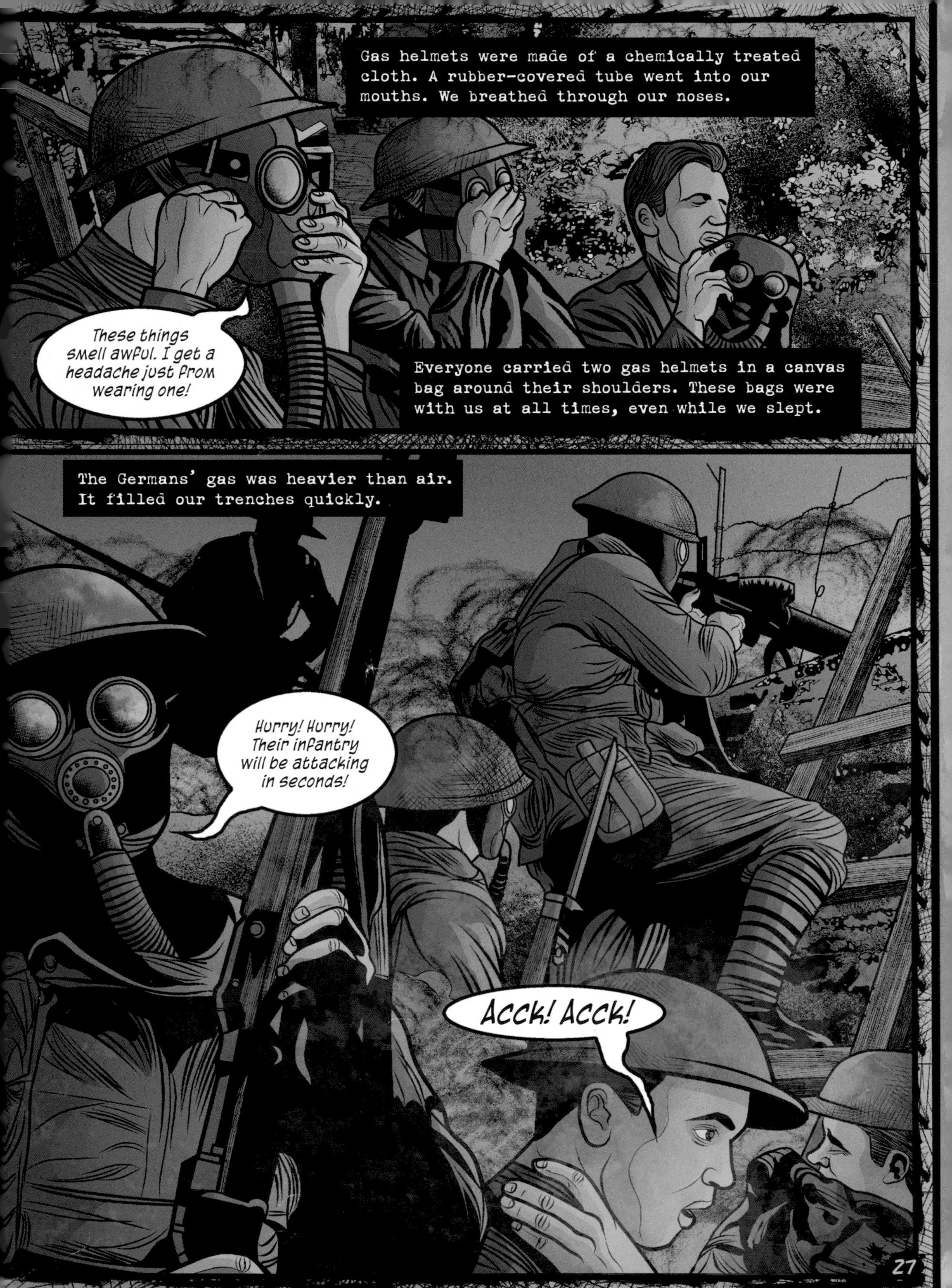
Gas helmets were made of a chemically treated cloth. A rubber-covered tube went into our mouths. We breathed through our noses.
These things smell awful. I get a headache just from wearing one!
Everyone carried two gas helmets in a canvas bag around their shoulders. These bags were with us at all times, even while we slept.
The Germans' gas was heavier than air. It filled our trenches quickly.
Hurry! Hurry! Their infantry will be attacking in seconds!
Acck! Acck!

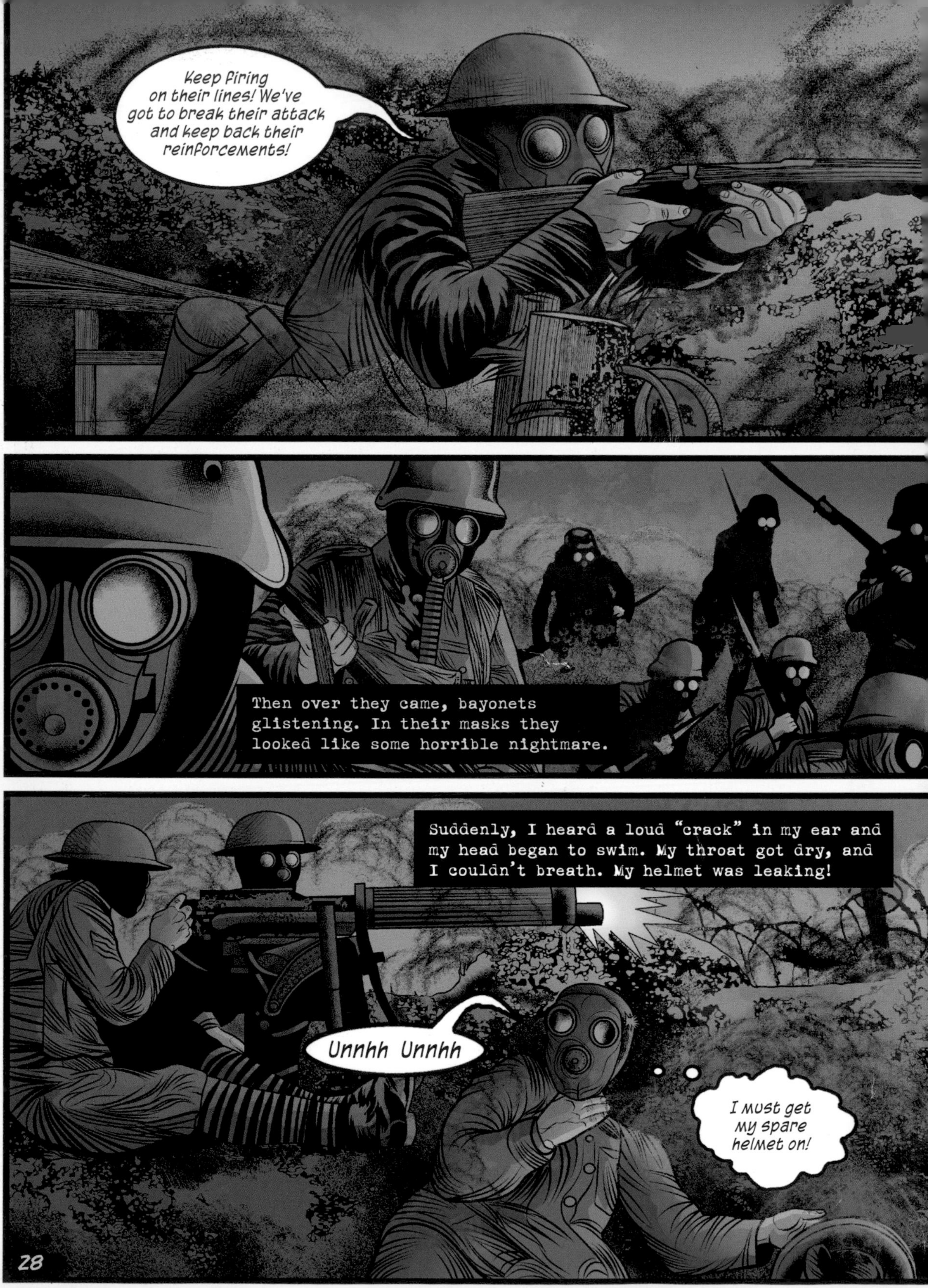
Keep firing on their lines! We've got to break their attack and keep back their reinforcements!
Then over they came, bayonets glistening. In their masks they looked like some horrible nightmare.
Suddenly, I heard a loud "crack" in my ear and my head began to swim. My throat got dry, and I couldn't breath. My helmet was leaking!
Unnhh Unnhh
I must get my spare helmet on!

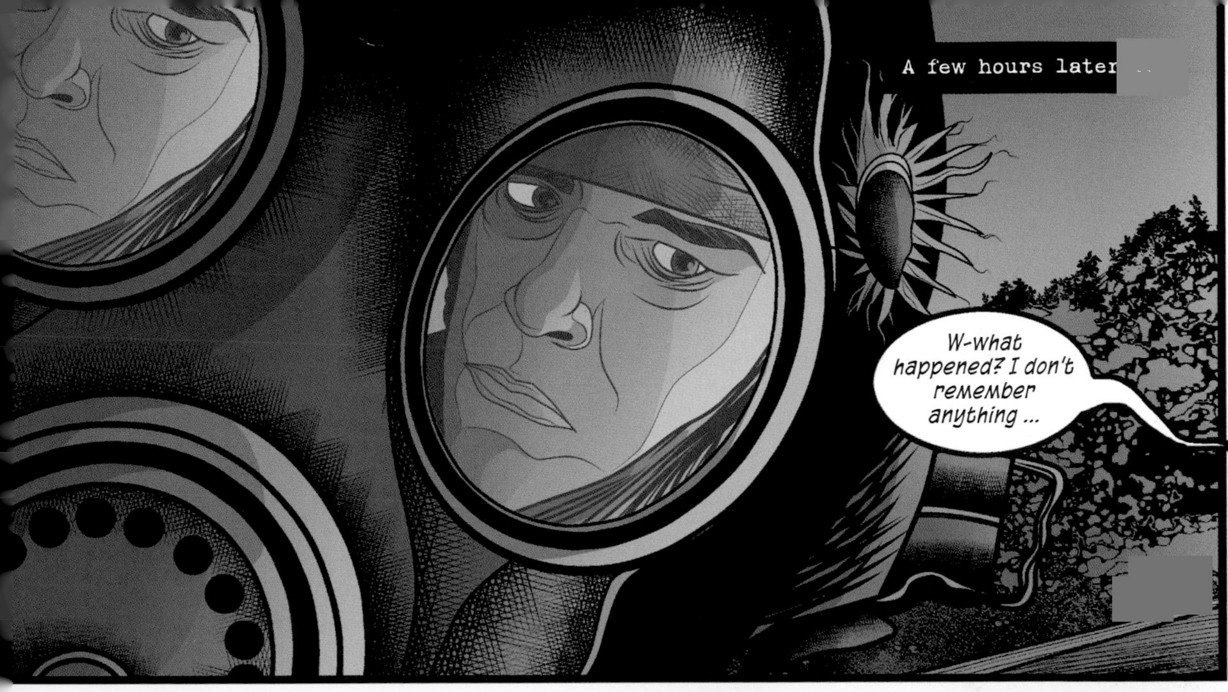
A few hours later . . .
W-what happened? I don't remember anything ...

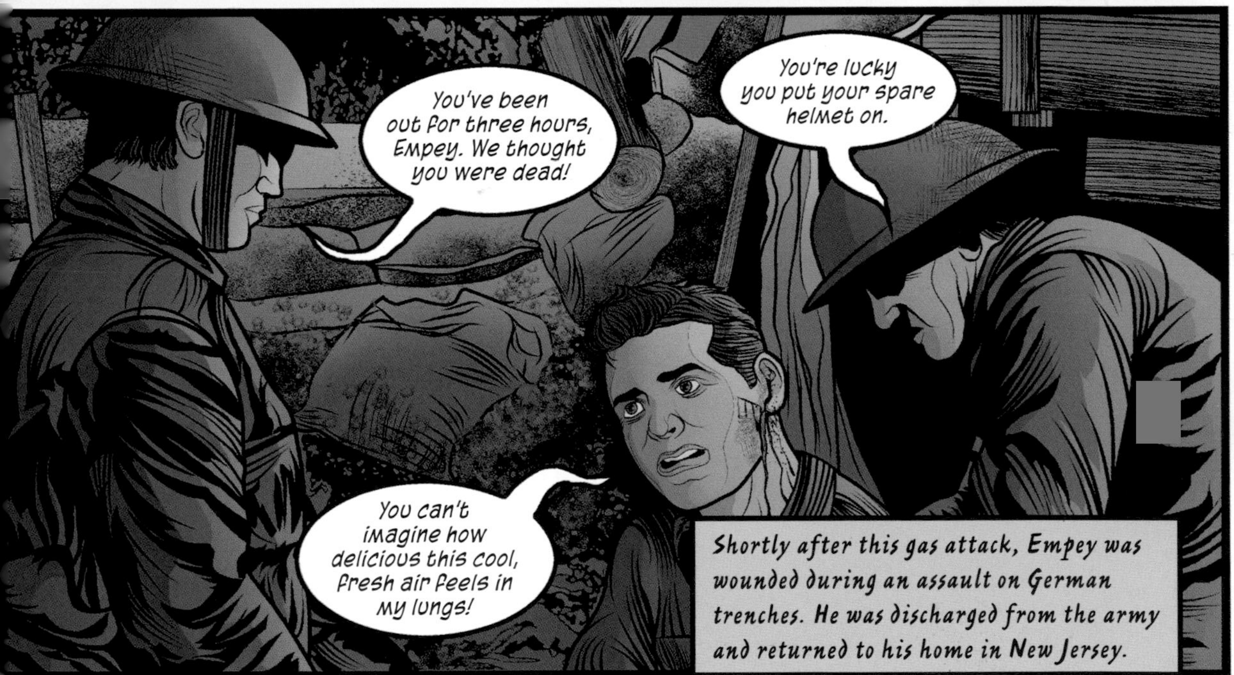
You've been out for three hours, Empey. We thought you were dead!
You're lucky you put your spare helmet on.
You can't imagine how delicious this cool, fresh air feels in my lungs!
Shortly after this gas attack, Empey was wounded during an assault on German trenches. He was discharged from the army and returned to his home in New Jersey.

Gas Warfare

Both sides used gas warfare in World War I. At first, cylinders filled with gas were placed along the front lines facing enemy trenches. The cylinders were opened, and winds carried the gas into enemy positions. Later, gas was put into artillery shells and shot at the enemy. Chlorine gas attacked the lungs, taking away the victim's ability to breathe. Mustard gas attacked the skin. It burned its victims, causing terrible blisters, incredible pain, and sometimes death.

GLOSSARY

ALLIANCE (uh-LY-uhnts)—an agreement between nations or groups of people to work together

ARTILLERY (ar-TI-luhr-ee)—cannons and other large guns used during battles

ASSASSINATION (uh-sass-uh-NAY-shun)—the murder of someone who is well known or important

BARON (BA-ruhn)—a man of great power or influence in some field or activity

BATTALION (buh-TAL-yuhn)—a group of soldiers

BRIGADE (bri-GAYD)—a unit of an army, usually made up of two or more battalions

CIVILIAN (si-VIL-yuhn)—a person who is not in the military

MORTAR (MOR-tur)—a short cannon that fires shells or rockets high in the air

RENDEZVOUS (RON-duh-voo)—a French word meaning "a prearranged meeting"

SERGEANT (SAR-juhnt)—officer in charge of other patrol officers

STARBOARD (STAR-burd)—the right-hand side of a ship

TORPEDO (tor-PEE-doh)—an underwater missile

TRENCH (TRENCH)—a long, deep area cut into the ground with dirt piled up on one side

READ MORE

Barber, Nicola. *World War I.* Living Through. Chicago: Heinemann Library, 2012.

Gregory, Josh. *World War I.* Cornerstones of Freedom. New York: Children's Press, 2012.

Heinrichs, Ann. *Voices of World War I: Stories from the Trenches.* Voices of War. Mankato, Minn.: Capstone Press, 2011.

Samuels, Charlie. *Timeline of World War I.* Americans at War: A Gareth Stevens Timeline Series. New York: Gareth Stevens Pub., 2012.

INTERNET SITES

FactHound offers a safe, fun way to find Internet sites related to this book. All sites on FactHound have been researched by our staff.

Here's all you do:

Visit www.facthound.com

Type in this code: 9781429686259

Super-cool stuff!

Check out projects, games and lots more at
www.capstonekids.com

INDEX